The Best
of
Slovak Cooking

The Best
of
Slovak Cooking

BY
SYLVIA AND JOHN LORINC

Hippocrene Books, Inc.
New York

641.5943

ISBN 0-7818-0765-4

For information, address:
HIPPOCRENE BOOKS, INC.
171 Madison Avenue
New York, NY 10016

Cataloging-in-Publication Data available from the Library of Congress

Printed in the United States of America.

Table of Contents

INTRODUCTION ❧ vii

SOUPS ❧ 1

VEGETABLES & SIDE DISHES ❧ 27

MAIN DISHES ❧ 51

DESSERTS & BREADS ❧ 91

RECIPE INDEX ❧ 135

Introduction

Slovaks often say, "We do not live to eat, but we eat to live." Looking at the traditionally abundant and varied Slovak table, however, one would think the opposite.

Historically speaking, Slovaks were industrious, both in the fields and the kitchen, as far as food is concerned. Many of the Slovakia's impressive mountains give way to rolling hills and river valleys, where agriculture, winemaking, and livestock raising are practiced. Throughout Slovakia's agrarian history, its people developed traditional meals for holidays, religious festivals, seasons of the year, and many other celebrations.

Whatever the game-rich forests, fertile farm lands, rivers and lakes had to offer, Slovak cooks put to good use. From ingredients and resources as diverse as duck and chamomile, they produced a variety of dishes with nature's bounty and became quite adept at using the locally available fare to create inventive and nourishing dishes.

The Slovak diet relies heavily on meat, whether fresh or cured. Some families still raise chickens, geese, ducks, rabbits, pigs and pigeons. Families that raise pigs, slaughter one every several years in a traditional ritual. Almost all parts of the pig are used in the preparation of favorite dishes.

Bryndzové *halušky* (noodles with goat cheese) and spicy dishes including goulash are also widely enjoyed. Squares of smoked Carpathian mountain sheep-milk cheese, *ostiepok,* are a favorite, often served with a thick slice of whole-grain bread, cold smoked meat, and beer.

Aromatic caraway seeds have a fixed place in traditional Slovak dishes, and sour cream is another often used ingredient—as a flavoring or to thicken and enrich sauces. Like many other central European cuisines, fresh and dried mushrooms are a favorite, and add flavor to many of Slovakia's characteristic dishes.

Wine, beer, *slivovica* (plum brandy), and *borovicka* (drink derived from berries of the juniper tree), are popular beverages. Grapes are grown in Slovakia, and a wine-drinking heritage continues there.

Slovakia's rich soil is especially suited for growing superb crops of grain. Wheat, barley and rye are used to make some of the most famous national dishes like breads, dumplings and noodles. Slovak cooks are celebrated throughout Europe for their baked goods made with native flour, valued for its high quality.

Over the centuries, the Slovak kitchen was influenced by the neighboring Russian, Polish, German, Czech and Hungarian peoples. Variations of cabbage, beet, veal, spice and dumpling dishes are shared by all these countries.

It is in the Slovaks' nature to offer their guests the best food and drink in their homes. So given the opportunity, enjoy Slovak hospitality, eat drink and be merry.

Dobru Chut!

Soups

SLOVAK SOUP SAUCE
(*Zapražka*)

Zapražka (pronounced za-prrash-ka) is a soup thickener, and much more. It is a quick and easy way to add zest to any soup.

4 teaspoons butter
1 small onion, chopped
2 tablespoons flour

Melt butter in small saucepan. Add onion and fry until brown. Carefully stir in flour to prevent lumps. Add to any soup.

BARLEY SOUP
(Jačmenova Polievka)

1 cup barley
½ pound ham
1 cup navy beans
3 cups diced carrots
1 cup diced celery
2 medium onions, chopped
1 clove garlic, chopped fine
1 bay leaf
1 sprig parsley, chopped

Rinse barley well. Place barley, ham, and beans in a large pot, add 2 quarts water, and cook for 2 hours. Add carrots, celery, onions, garlic, and bay leaf, and simmer for 1 hour. Sprinkle parsley over soup before serving.

MAKES 6 SERVINGS

BEET SOUP
(Cviklova Polievka)

7 tender young beets
juice of 1 lemon
1 teaspoon sugar
salt to taste
1 cup sour cream

Peel and wash beets, and cut into small cubes. Place in
medium pot, add 1 quart water, and boil until beets are soft.
Add lemon juice, sugar, and salt. Boil an additional 5 minutes,
remove from heat, and thoroughly stir in sour cream, and
serve. Soup can be served hot or cold.

MAKES 4 SERVINGS

CARAWAY SEED SOUP
(Kmínova Polievka)

1 tablespoon caraway seeds
salt to taste
1 tablespoon butter
1 tablespoon flour

In a large pot, simmer caraway seeds in 4 cups salted, warm water for 10 minutes. In a small skillet, melt butter, add flour and brown. Stir in 1 cup cold water, and bring to a boil. Add to caraway seed water, and boil for about 3 minutes. Soup is ready to serve. If desired, seeds can be strained out before serving.

MAKES 4 SERVINGS

CAULIFLOWER SOUP
(Karfiolová Polievka)

1 medium cauliflower (broken or cut into
        bite-size pieces)
1 carrot, diced
salt and pepper to taste
zapražka (page 3)
2 egg yolks
½ cup milk

Add cauliflower, carrot, and 2 quarts water to a large pot.
Cook for approximately 30 minutes. Add salt, pepper, and
zapražka to pot, and cook for 3 minutes. Place egg yolks and
milk in small mixing bowl and mix thoroughly. Add contents to
pot and cook 1 minute.

MAKES 6 SERVINGS

CELERY SOUP
(Zelerová Polievka)

1 large onion, chopped
¼ teaspoon paprika
2 tablespoons butter
1 stalk celery, chopped fine
4 chicken livers, cut into small pieces
pepper to taste
1 clove garlic, minced
zapražka (page 3)
salt to taste

Add onion, paprika, and butter to a large pot. Sauté onion until brown, and add celery and liver and sauté for an additional 10 minutes. Add pepper, garlic, and 2 quarts water. When celery is soft, add *zapražka* and cook for an additional 2 to 3 minutes. Salt and serve.

MAKES 6 SERVINGS

DILL SOUP
(Koprová Polievka)

6 long dill stalks
2 tablespoons butter
dash of paprika
salt and pepper to taste
dash of powdered caraway
zapražka (page 3)

Chop dill stalks into tiny segments. Melt butter in small frying pan, and sauté dill for 10 minutes. In a medium-size pot, add 1 quart water, paprika, salt, pepper, and caraway, and bring to a boil. Add dill and *zapražka* into pot, and cook for 5 minutes.

MAKES 6 SERVINGS

MUSHROOM SOUP
(Hríbova Polievka)

1 pound mushrooms
4 ounces sauerkraut juice
salt and pepper to taste
zapražka (page 3)

Rinse mushrooms in cold water, chop into small pieces, and put into a medium-size pot. Add 1 quart water and boil for 20 minutes. Add sauerkraut juice, salt, pepper, and boil for 5 minutes. Add *zapražka*, and simmer for 2 minutes. Serve hot.

MAKES 4 SERVINGS

KALE SOUP
(Kelová Polievka)

8 ounces fresh kale, cut into bite-size pieces
    (Spinach can be substituted for kale)
4 small potatoes, cubed
1 clove garlic, pressed
dash of paprika
salt and pepper to taste
zapražka (page 3)

Add kale, potatoes, garlic, paprika, salt, pepper, and 2 quarts water to a large pot. Bring to a boil, and simmer for 25 minutes. Add *zapražka*, mix well, and simmer for additional 2 to 3 minutes. Thin slices of sausage or hot dogs can be added for a meat dish.

MAKES 6 SERVINGS

KOHLRABI SOUP
(Kalerábova Polievka)

2 medium kohlrabi
1 small potato
salt and pepper to taste
zapražka (page 3)

Peel kohlrabi and potato, and cut into small cubes. Put into medium-size pot, add 1 quart water, and simmer for 40 minutes. Add salt, pepper, and *zapražka* to soup, and simmer for 2 minutes. Serve hot.

MAKES 4 SERVINGS

SOUR CABBAGE SOUP
(Kysla Kapustná Polievka)

1 medium head cabbage
5 black peppercorns
2 bay leaves
4 ounces sauerkraut juice
zapražka (page 3)

Wash and cut cabbage into small pieces. Place cabbage, peppercorns, bay leaves, and 2 quarts water into large pot, and cook for 35 minutes. Add sauerkraut juice and *zapražka*, and cook for additional 5 minutes. If soup is too sour, add 1 teaspoon sugar. Serve with dark bread.

MAKES 6 SERVINGS

TOMATO SOUP
(Paradajkova Polievka)

½ cup white rice
6 large tomatoes
salt and pepper to taste
1 clove garlic, diced
zapražka (page 3)

Put rice and 1 cup water into a large pot. Bring to a boil,
then turn to simmer, cover, and cook for 15 minutes. Steam
tomatoes and remove skin and core (or use canned tomatoes).
Add tomatoes and 2 quarts water into large pot and cook for
10 minutes. Add salt, pepper, garlic, and *zapražka*, and cook
for 2 minutes. Add cooked rice and serve.

MAKES 6 SERVINGS

ONION SOUP WITH COTTAGE CHEESE
(Cibuľová S Syrom)

8 ounces bacon
6 large onions, chopped
4 caraway seeds
salt to taste
4 beef bouillon cubes
1 cup cottage cheese
1 cup milk
2 sprigs parsley

Fry bacon with onions in large skillet. Add caraway seeds and salt to skillet, and set aside. Add bouillon cubes and 1 quart water to large pot and cook until cubes dissolve. Add contents of skillet to pot, and cook for 10 minutes. Place cottage cheese into cheesecloth and squeeze water from cheese. Add cheese and milk into mixing bowl and beat until smooth. Add mixture to soup. Sprinkle parsley into soup, and serve with dark bread.

MAKES 6 SERVINGS

POTATO SOUP
(Zemiakova Polievka)

3 large potatoes
1 stalk celery, diced
2 medium onions, diced
2 carrots, diced
1 sprig parsley, chopped fine
salt and pepper to taste
1 cup milk
zapražka (page 3)

Place potatoes, celery, onions, carrots, and parsley in large pot and cover with 2 quarts water. Add salt and pepper, and cook until tender (about 25 minutes). Add milk and *zapražka*, and cook until soup thickens.

MAKES 6 SERVINGS

GREEN BEAN SOUP (FRESH)
(Stručková Fazulová Polievka)

1 pound fresh green beans
1 large clove garlic, diced
dash of paprika
salt and pepper to taste
zapražka (page 3)
2 tablespoons sour cream

Remove tips from both ends of green beans, and wash in cold water. Cut beans into 1-inch pieces. Add beans and 2 quarts water to a large pot and bring to boil. Cook for 15 minutes. Add garlic, paprika, salt, pepper, and *zapražka*, and cook for additional 3 minutes. Add sour cream and you are ready to serve.

MAKES 6 SERVINGS

NATURAL VEGETABLE SOUP
(Prírodná Zeleninová Polievka)

1 kohlrabi
2 carrots
1 sprig parsley
1 stalk celery
1 tablespoon green peas
4 leaves kale
15 pods green beans
4 small potatoes
1 onion
1 clove garlic
zapražka (page 3)
dash of paprika
salt and pepper to taste

Clean and wash kohlrabi, carrots, parsley, celery, peas, kale, beans, potatoes, onion, garlic, and cut into cubes, place in large pot, add 2 quarts water, and cook for 20 minutes. Add *zapražka*, paprika, salt, pepper, and cook for an additional 3 minutes. Serve with noodles and dark bread.

MAKES 6 SERVINGS

DRY BEAN SOUP
(Fazuľova Polievka)

1 pound dried beans
2 cloves garlic
salt and pepper to taste
zapražka (page 3)
½ cup sour cream

In a large pot, add 2 quarts water and the beans, and let sit overnight. Add garlic, salt, and pepper, and cook for 1½ hours. Add *zapražka*, and mix. Add sour cream to serving bowl, and serve with dark bread.

MAKES 6 SERVINGS

LENTIL SOUP
(Šošovicova Polievka)

1 pound lentils
2 cloves garlic
zapražka (page 3)
salt and pepper to taste
3 tablespoons sour cream

Rinse lentils, place in large pot, and add 2 quarts water. Add
garlic and simmer for 45 minutes. Add *zapražka*, and salt
and pepper to taste. Remove from heat, add sour cream, and
serve. (Note: lentils could be replaced with split peas, however
if you use peas, you must cook for only 25 minutes.)

MAKES 6 SERVINGS

GARLIC SOUP
(Cesnaková Polievka)

2 tablespoons butter
4 cloves garlic, minced
1 quart chicken bouillon
salt and pepper to taste
dash of paprika

Over low heat, melt butter in a medium pot, and sauté garlic until golden brown. Add bouillon, salt, pepper, and paprika, and simmer for 10 minutes. Serve with dark bread.

MAKES 4 SERVINGS

CHICKEN VEGETABLE SOUP WITH DUMPLINGS
(Slepačia Polievka s Knedličkami)

DUMPLINGS:
liver of 1 chicken
½ teaspoon salt
1 egg
3 tablespoons flour

Heat a medium pot of water to a boil. To make the dumplings, in a small bowl, scrape chicken liver to form small particles, add salt, egg, and flour to make a soft dough. Knead dough until uniform. Scoop mixture with a teaspoon into boiling water to form dumplings. Cook until they float, then remove, rinse, and set aside.

SOUP:

1 onion, chopped
3 tablespoons butter, melted
1 small chicken cut into small pieces
    (retain liver for dumplings)
dash of pepper
1 tablespoon salt
1 tablespoon paprika
1 kohlrabi, or small head of cabbage,
    shredded
1 sprig parsley, chopped
1 stalk celery, chopped
1 green pepper, chopped
1 tomato, chopped
2 carrots, chopped
½ cup rice

Sauté onion in butter until golden brown. Add chicken pieces. Add pepper, salt, paprika, kohlrabi, parsley, celery, green pepper, tomato, and carrots. Cover with 2 cups of water. Simmer gently for about 30 minutes, or until chicken and vegetables are cooked. In a separate pot, heat 6 cups of water, add rice, and bring to a boil. Reduce heat and simmer until rice is cooked, about 45 minutes. Combine chicken, vegetables, and dumplings with rice, and serve.

MAKES 4 TO 6 SERVINGS

BEEF SOUP
(Hovädzia Polievka)

½ pound chuck (plus bone)
3 stalks celery, thinly sliced
5 sprigs parsley, chopped
1 medium onion, chopped
2 carrots, thinly sliced
1 small potato, cubed
1 small clove garlic, minced
6 whole peppercorns
salt and pepper to taste
dash of paprika

Rinse meat and bone in cold water. Place meat and bone in large pot and add 1½ quarts water. Bring to boil and then simmer for 1 hour. Dispose of foam and scum from surface of simmering liquid. Add celery, parsley, onion, carrots, potato, and garlic, and continue simmering until meat is tender. Add peppercorns, salt, pepper, and paprika. Serve with noodles.

MAKES 6 SERVINGS

HAM BONE PEA SOUP
(Hrachova Polievka)

1 large ham bone
1 pound split peas
1 stalk celery, chopped
1 sprig parsley, chopped
1 onion, chopped
zpražka (page 3)
1 cup milk

In a large pot, add ham bone, peas, celery, parsley, onion, and 2 quarts water, and cook for 30 minutes. Remove bone and dispose. Prepare *zapražka*, add to pot, and cook for 3 minutes. Add milk, mix, and cook for another 2 minutes. Serve with croutons, grated cheese, or garlic bread.

MAKES 6 SERVINGS

FISH SOUP
(Rybacia Polievka)

1 pound fresh fish (preferably carp)
1 medium onion, chopped
1 stalk celery, thinly sliced
1 carrot, thinly sliced
1 sprig parsley, chopped
4 mushrooms, diced
1 clove garlic, minced
salt and pepper to taste
3 tablespoons sour cream
2 tablespoons flour

Clean and remove bones from fish, and cut into bite-size pieces. Add fish, 1 quart cold water, and onion to large pot, and bring to boil. Cook for 5 minutes, or until fish is soft. Remove fish and set aside. Strain soup into another pot. Into this pot, add celery, carrots, parsley, mushrooms, garlic, salt, and pepper. Cook until celery is tender. Add fish to soup. In a separate bowl, mix sour cream and flour until all lumps are removed. Add to soup and cook for 2 minutes.

MAKES 6 SERVINGS

Vegetables
&
Side Dishes

APPLES WITH HORSERADISH
(Jablká S Chrenom)

4 tart apples
4 to 5 tablespoons grated horseradish
¾ teaspoon sugar

Grate apples into bowl containing horseradish and sugar. Blend while grating to prevent discoloration of apples. Add more sugar if too tart or if horseradish is too strong.

MAKES 40 SERVINGS (1 TABLESPOON PER SERVING)

BAKED CAULIFLOWER
(Pečený Karfiol)

2 large cauliflowers
1 tablespoon butter
1 cup bread crumbs
2 cups baked ham, cut into cubes
½ cup sour cream
2 eggs
salt and pepper to taste
½ cup grated cheese

Preheat over to 350°F. Clean cauliflower, place in large pot, and boil in 2 quarts water with ¼ teaspoon salt for 10 minutes. Coat baking dish with butter and bread crumbs. Remove cauliflower from water and place in baking dish. Sprinkle ham over cauliflower. In a bowl, mix sour cream, eggs, salt, and pepper. First pour mixture over cauliflower, then sprinkle cheese over mixture. Bake for 25 minutes. Serve with dark or Italian bread, or mashed potatoes.

MAKES 6 SERVINGS

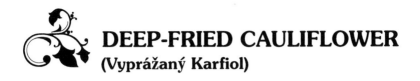

DEEP-FRIED CAULIFLOWER
(Vyprážaný Karfiol)

4 small cauliflowers (cut into 1½-inch pieces)
3 tablespoons flour
2 eggs
½ cup milk
1 cup bread crumbs
dash of salt
2 cups vegetable oil

Clean cauliflower and cook in 1 quart water with ¼ teaspoon salt for 5 minutes (cauliflower should not be fully cooked). Pour cauliflower into colander and let cool. Use 3 mixing bowls: add flour to the first one, mix eggs and milk in the second bowl, and add bread crumbs and salt to the third bowl. Piece by piece, coat cauliflower with flour, egg/milk mixture, and bread crumbs. Heat oil in large skillet, and deep fry the cauliflower until golden brown. Serve with french fries.

MAKES 6 SERVINGS

DEEP-FRIED CHEESE
(Vyprážaný Syr)

½ cup flour
2 eggs
½ cup bread crumbs
4 slices of any hard cheese (¼ inch thick)
2 cups vegetable oil

Prepare 3 bowls: add flour to the first bowl, mix eggs in the second bowl, and add bread crumbs to the third bowl. Coat the cheese with flour, then dip each slice into the egg mixture, then coat the cheese with bread crumbs. Heat oil in a large skillet and quickly fry cheese on both sides. Must be served hot. Serve with french fries or mashed potatoes.

MAKES 4 SERVINGS

EASTER CHEESE
(Veľkonočný Syr)

1 quart milk
12 eggs
1 teaspoon salt

Pour milk into saucepan, and break eggs (1 at a time) into milk. Add salt and mix slowly. Cook in a double boiler, stir constantly, and when mixture begins to look like scrambled eggs, pour into cheesecloth (draped over large pot), and tie so that a tight ball of egg is formed. Press on ball to drain all liquid from egg mass. Hang cheesecloth to allow drainage for 1 hour. Carefully remove cheesecloth so as to prevent breakage, and refrigerate for minimum of 3 hours. Serve as a side dish.

MAKES 12 SERVINGS

DUMPLINGS
(Haluška)

3½ cups flour
dash of salt
2 large egg yolks

In a large mixing bowl, add flour and salt, and mix. Add egg
yolks, and slowly add approximately 1 cup water while mixing,
taking care that dough is thin, but not watery. Place dough on
board. Add 3 cups water to large pot and bring to boil. Dip
butter knife in boiling water, and cut small pieces of dough and
push into boiling water. Dumplings are done when they float
on surface of water. Drain in colander, and rinse in cold water
to prevent sticking. Serve with butter and/or poppy seeds,
boiled cabbage, or cottage cheese and bacon bits.

MAKES 4 SERVINGS

DUMPLINGS WITH FETA CHEESE
(Bryndzové Halušky)

1½ pounds raw potatoes
2¾ cups whole wheat flour
salt
½ pound feta cheese
butter
¼ pound smoked bacon

Peel and grate the potatoes and mix with flour in a large bowl. Add salt to taste. Dumplings are formed by scooping the mixture (with a spoon or knife) into boiling, salted water. Dumplings should be about ½-inch. (To prevent sticking, dip the scooper into boiling water). The dumplings are cooked when they float to the surface. When the dumplings are cooked, remove, drain in colander, and rinse with cold water.

To make bryndza, rinse the feta in cold water, grate, and mix with soft butter to the consistency of soft cream cheese.

Fry bacon and cut into small pieces. Mix with the bryndza and dumplings, and serve.

MAKES 4 SERVINGS

POTATO DUMPLINGS
(Zemiakova Knedla)

2 cups mashed potatoes
2 tablespoons butter
1 tablespoon chopped onion
1 egg
¾ cup flour
dash of salt and pepper
1 cup bread cubes (¼ inch)

In a large bowl, mix potatoes and 1 tablespoon butter. Add onion, egg, flour, salt & pepper, and mix well. In a small skillet, sauté bread cubes in remaining tablespoon butter until golden brown. Form balls the size of an egg by covering 4 bread cubes with potatoes. In a medium pot, bring 2 quarts water to a boil, and gently add potato balls, and cook for 7 minutes. Remove balls with strainer, and place on serving platter. Serve with any meat dish, or with melted butter.

MAKES 6 SERVINGS

EGG NOODLES
(Slíže)

3 eggs
1 teaspoon salt
1 tablespoon butter
2 cups flour

Combine eggs and salt in a medium bowl, and beat until foamy. Melt butter in a small skillet, and add to bowl. Slowly add flour to bowl, and mix into a stiff dough. Divide into 2 balls. Place on floured board, and roll into a thin sheet. Let dry for about 20 minutes. With a sharp knife, cut the dough into 2-inch-wide strips. Stack the strips 4 layers high. Cut noodles to desired width. Add noodles to boiling water, and cook for 3 minutes or until tender. Pour into colander and rinse with cold water. Serve in soup, or with poppy seeds and sugar, or with scrambled eggs. (If noodles are to be used at a later time, they must be thoroughly dried after cutting.)

MAKES 4 SERVINGS

FRIED LETTUCE
(Vyprážaný Šalát)

1 head romaine lettuce (or 2 heads
  other lettuce)
½ pound bacon

Wash lettuce and cut into bite-size pieces. In a large skillet, cut bacon into small pieces and fry until crispy. Place lettuce in skillet, and sauté for 3 minutes. Serve hot.

MAKES 4 SERVINGS

LAYERED POTATO CASSEROLE
(Nakladané Zemiaky)

8 potatoes
6 eggs
½ stick (4 tablespoons) butter
salt and pepper

Boil potatoes and eggs in same pot for 20 minutes. Peel and slice potatoes and eggs. Preheat oven to 350°F. Coat a bread pan with 2 tablespoons of butter, and place alternate layers of potatoes and eggs to a depth of about 3-inches. Spread remaining 2 tablespoons butter on top and bake for 45 minutes. Season with salt and pepper. Serve as is, or with sour cream.

MAKES 4 TO 6 SERVINGS

POTATO PANCAKES
(Zemiakova Baba)

6 potatoes
½ cup flour
1 egg
salt and pepper
2 small cloves garlic
oil

Peel and grate potatoes. In a large bowl, add potatoes, flour, egg, salt, pepper, and garlic, and mix well. Cover bottom of frying pan with cooking oil, and heat. Scoop mixture into hot oil, spread to thickness of dinner plate, and fry each side until golden brown. Serve plain, or with sour cream.

MAKES 4 SERVINGS

POTATO SALAD
(Zemiakový Šalát)

8 potatoes
2 carrots
1 stalk celery
½ cup green peas
2 medium apples, cubed
2 hard boiled eggs, cubed
2 sour pickles, cubed
1 small onion, chopped
1 cup mayonnaise
½ cup sour cream
salt and pepper to taste

Wash potatoes and cook them in a large pot for 20 minutes.
After the potatoes are cooked (with skins), cut them into
cubes. In a separate pot, cook carrots and celery for 20
minutes, then cut them into cubes. In a bowl, combine the
potatoes, carrots, and celery, with peas, apples, eggs, pickles,
onion, mayonnaise, and sour cream. Mix well, and place in
refrigerator for 30 minutes. Season with salt and pepper.
Serve as a side dish.

MAKES 6 SERVINGS

POTATO STEW
(Zemiakový Guláš)

8 potatoes
½ stick (4 tablespoons) butter
1 large onion, chopped fine
⅓ cup flour
salt and pepper to taste
½ cup sour cream
zapražka (page 3)

Peel potatoes, cut into bite-size pieces, and boil in salted water until fully cooked. Do not drain.

Add *zapražka* to potatoes and water, and cook until *guláš* thickens. Serve as is, with sour cream, or garnish with paprika.

MAKES 4 TO 6 SERVINGS

MUSHROOM PAPRIKAS
(Hríbový Paprikáš)

1 pound mushrooms, sliced (about 4 cups)
1 medium onion, chopped
1 tablespoon butter
½ teaspoon paprika
salt and pepper to taste
1 quart beef bouillon
¾ cup sour cream
1 tablespoon flour

Wash mushrooms and sauté with onions and butter in
large skillet. Add paprika and mix well. Add salt, pepper,
and bouillon. Cook for 10 minutes. Mix sour cream with flour,
and add to skillet. Cook for 4 more minutes. Serve with rice
or pasta.

MAKES 4 SERVINGS

PAGACH
(Pagáč)

PAGACH FILLING:
½ pound sauerkraut
2 tablespoons butter
2 tablespoons sugar
pinch of salt
pinch of cinnamon

1 cake yeast, or 1 envelope
1 cup boiled milk
1 tablespoon butter
1 tablespoon sugar
5¼ cups all-purpose flour
2 teaspoons salt
2 egg yolks, lightly beaten
cream, butter, and sugar for topping

To make filling, wash sauerkraut in ½ cup water, and squeeze dry. Chop fine. Sauté in butter with sugar and cinnamon until brown. Cool to lukewarm.

To make pagach, dissolve yeast in ½ cup warm water. Pour ½ cup boiled milk over butter and sugar. Cool to lukewarm, and add dissolved yeast. Sift flour and salt into deep bowl, and add egg yolks and yeast mixture with remaining ½ cup boiled milk, and an additional ½ cup water, and knead well. Cover with cloth and set aside in warm, draft-free place to rise for about 2 hours, or until dough has doubled in size. Turn out on floured board, and divide into 3 equal portions. Cover each portion with a bowl and let rest for 10 minutes. Take one piece at a time, turn over on board, and flatten the center with the back of your hand. Place filling in center and draw up and pinch edges together. Again place bowl over dough for 10 minutes. Preheat oven to 375 °F. Do the following steps on each of the 3 pieces:

1. Turn dough over and press carefully with back of hand all around.

2. With a floured rolling pin, roll out slowly, so the filling will not break through, until the dough is 12 inches in diameter.

3. Place both hands under pagach and put in bottom of the oven for 10 minutes.

4. Remove pagach, turn over, and place on rack in center of oven, and bake another 10 minutes.

5. When done, wrap in damp cloth, and let stand for 10 minutes.

6. Brush lightly with sweet cream, then with butter on both sides.

7. Cut to desired size, sprinkle with sugar, and serve.

MAKES 4 TO 6 SERVINGS

PIROGIS
(Pirohy)

FILLINGS:

Cottage Cheese
½ cup cottage cheese
1 egg yolk
1 teaspoon butter

Use cheesecloth to remove excess liquid from cottage cheese. In a small mixing bowl, add dry cheese, egg yolk, and butter, and mix.

Mashed Potatoes
2 large potatoes
1 tablespoon butter
dash of salt

Peel potatoes, cut into sections, cook until tender, drain, and mash. Add butter and salt, and mix. Let cool before stuffing pirogis.

Sauerkraut
1 tablespoon butter
1 cup sauerkraut

In a small skillet, melt butter, and sauté sauerkraut for 10 minutes. Let cool before stuffing pirogis.

PIROGIS:

1 cup flour
1 egg
¼ teaspoon salt
melted butter to taste

In a large bowl, add flour, egg, salt, ¼ cup cold water, and mix until soft, uniform dough is formed. Place dough on floured board and roll until thin (about ⅛ inch thick). With a sharp knife, cut into squares (about 3 inches by 3 inches). Place filling into center of square, fold into triangle shape, and pinch edges shut. In a large pot, bring 2 quarts water to a boil, drop pirogis into water, and cook until all pirogis are floating. Pour into colander, and rinse with cold water. Place in serving bowl, add melted butter, and serve.

MAKES 2 SERVINGS

SALSA WITH EGGS
(Lešo S Vajcami)

2 tablespoons butter
1 large onion, chopped
2 tomatoes, chopped
1 bell pepper, chopped
1 clove garlic, chopped
kielbasa (6-inch link), chopped
4 eggs

Melt butter in a large skillet, and sauté onion until golden brown. Add tomatoes, bell pepper, garlic, kielbasa, and sauté for an additional 5 minutes. Break eggs in bowl and add to skillet. Stir and cook for 3 minutes. Serve with dark bread.

MAKES 2 SERVINGS

SWEET AND SOUR RED CABBAGE
(Kyslo Sladká Kapusta)

½ stick (4 tablespoons) butter
1 medium onion, chopped
1 teaspoon salt
1 small head red cabbage, chopped
1 tablespoon sugar
¼ cup cider vinegar

Melt butter in a large pot, add onion, and sauté for 5 minutes. Add salt, ½ cup water, cabbage, sugar, and vinegar, cover pot and simmer for 30 minutes, or until cabbage is soft. Serve with hot dogs or kielbasa, and dark bread.

MAKES 4 SERVINGS

Main Dishes

BAKED GOOSE
(Pečená Hus)

1 medium goose, thoroughly washed
    (remove organs)
1 tablespoon salt
dash of caraway seeds
1 cup sour cream

Place the goose in a large pan, sprinkle salt uniformly over the goose, and refrigerate for 4 hours. Preheat oven to 350°F. Add 2 cups water, and sprinkle caraway seeds over goose. Bake for 1 hour. Discard water, cover goose with sour cream, raise oven temperature to 400°F, and bake for 20 minutes. Serve with rice.

MAKES 8 SERVINGS

ROAST DUCK
(Pečená Kačica)

1 duck
1 large onion, whole

Preheat oven to 325°F. Wash duck well in warm water, and insert onion inside duck. Pour 1 cup hot water on duck. Bake for 1½ hours, basting duck often. Remove and discard onion and drippings. Serve with rice, stuffing, or baked potatoes.

MAKES 6 SERVINGS

BREADED CHICKEN
(Vyprážaná Sliepka)

8 parts (breasts or thighs) chicken
2 eggs
salt and pepper to taste
3 tablespoons milk
½ cup flour
1½ cup bread crumbs
1 pound shortening (preferably Crisco)

Wash chicken and remove all skin. Dry chicken with a cloth or paper towel. In a bowl beat eggs, add salt and pepper, and slowly stir the milk into this mixture. Place the flour and bread crumbs on separate flat plates. Coat the chicken parts with flour, dip in egg mixture, and coat with bread crumbs. Heat shortening in a frying pan. Don't add chicken parts until shortening is hot. This prevents the chicken from absorbing shortening. Fry, and turn the chicken, until both sides are golden brown. Remove from fryer and place on paper towels to remove excess grease.

MAKES 4 TO 6 SERVINGS

CHICKEN PAPRIKA
(Slepačí Paprikaš)

1 medium-size onion, chopped
4 tablespoons shortening
1 tablespoon paprika
1 tablespoon salt
½ teaspoon black pepper
4 to 5 pounds chicken parts
1 cup sour cream

In large frying pan, brown onion in shortening. Add paprika, salt, pepper, and chicken. Simmer for 10 minutes. Add 1½ cups water, cover, cook until tender. Remove chicken and place in large bowl. Add sour cream to frying pan, and mix well. Pour sauce over chicken, and serve with rice or dumplings (page 34).

MAKES 4 TO 6 SERVINGS

NITRA DELICATESSEN
(Nitrianska Pochút'ka)

1 pound boneless, skinless, chicken breasts
½ stick (4 tablespoons) butter
¼ cup sugar
½ pound seedless grapes
3 apples, diced
½ cup white wine
1 cup chopped nuts
juice of ½ lemon

Tenderize chicken breasts with wooden mallet. Place chicken in large skillet with butter, and sauté for 10 minutes. In another pan, add ¼ cup water, and sugar, and heat for 5 minutes. To this pan, add grapes, apples, and white wine, and sauté for 5 minutes. Place chicken on serving platter, scoop fruit mix on top of the chicken, sprinkle with nuts and lemon juice. Serve with rice.

MAKES 4 SERVINGS

CHICKEN LIVERS WITH RICE
(Slepačia Pečienka s Ryžou)

2 tablespoons butter
1 large onion, chopped
4 chicken livers, chopped
1 cup uncooked rice, rinsed
salt and pepper to taste

In a medium pot, melt butter and sauté onion until brown. Add chicken livers, 1 cup water, and simmer for 5 minutes. In a large pot, add rice, 4 cups water, and boil for 10 minutes. Combine contents of medium pot with rice, and cook for 45 minutes. Add salt and pepper, and meal is ready to serve.

MAKES 4 SERVINGS

CABBAGE-HAM-NOODLE CASSEROLE
(Kapusta S Šunkou A Slížami)

1 medium head cabbage
5 tablespoons butter
dash of salt
½ pound wide egg noodles
½ pound ham, cut into cubes

Wash cabbage, cut into bite-size pieces, and remove and discard core. Add cabbage to large pot with 1 tablespoon butter, 1 cup water, and salt, and boil for 20 minutes, or until cabbage is soft. In another pot, add 2 quarts water and noodles, and cook until soft. Drain noodles in colander and rinse with cold water. In a large skillet, add 4 tablespoons butter, ham, and noodles, and fry until golden brown. Add cabbage (taking care to drain water) to skillet and mix with ham and noodles, and cook for 1 additional minute. Serve with pickles.

MAKES 6 SERVINGS

HAM ROLLS
(Šunkovy Závitok)

1 tablespoon horseradish
1 pound ham, sliced ¼ inch thick
2 tablespoons flour
2 eggs
½ cup bread crumbs
1 cup vegetable oil

Spread horseradish over each slice of ham, roll into a
tight cylinder, and fasten with toothpicks or string. Set up
3 medium-size bowls: add flour to the first, add beaten eggs to
the second, and add bread crumbs to the third. Dip each ham
roll into each of the bowls starting with the flour bowl, and
ending with the bread crumbs. Heat oil in a medium skillet, fry
ham rolls until brown, then place on absorbent paper to absorb
excess oil. Serve with mashed potatoes or dark bread.

MAKES 6 SERVINGS

ZVOLEN SMOKED HAM
(Zvolen Údené)

½ pound dry beans
1 pound smoked ham
1 stalk celery, chopped
1 large onion, chopped
salt and pepper to taste
½ cup olive or peanut oil
2 tablespoons vinegar
1 tablespoon mustard
2 dill pickles, chopped
1 teaspoon sugar
2 hard-boiled eggs

In a large pot, add beans and 2 quarts water, and let sit overnight. Add ham to pot, and cook for 2½ hours. Remove beans and ham and discard water. Add beans, ham, celery, onion, salt, pepper, oil, vinegar, mustard, pickles, and sugar to pot. Mix well, and arrange on serving plate. Slice eggs and decorate serving plate, and serve.

MAKES 6 SERVINGS

JELLIED PIG'S FEET
(Huspenina)

4 pounds pig's feet
1 tablespoon salt
6 whole black peppercorns
1 onion with skin
1 clove garlic, chopped
¼ teaspoon paprika
pepper to taste

Scrub pigs feet in warm water, place in large pot, and cover with 2 quarts water. Bring to boil and skim and discard foam. Lower heat and add salt, peppercorns, onion, garlic, and paprika. Cook 5 hours (meat will separate from bones). Strain, and pour liquid into soup bowls. Remove bones, cut meat into bite-size pieces, and add to soup bowls. Cool, then place in refrigerator overnight (liquid will jell). Sprinkle with paprika, salt, and pepper before serving.

MAKES 6 SERVINGS

KIELBASA WITH SAUERKRAUT AND POTATOES
(Klobasy s Kyslou Kapustou a Zemiakmi)

2 pounds kielbasa, cut into 1-inch sections
1 pound sauerkraut
½ pouch powdered onion soup
4 large potatoes, peeled and cubed

Preheat oven to 350°F. In a large baking pan, add kielbasa, sauerkraut, onion soup, and potatoes. Bake for 1 hour.

MAKES 5 SERVINGS

SHEPHERD'S KIELBASA
(Bačovská Klobasa)

1 pound potatoes, peeled and boiled
2 eggs
1 cup flour
dash of salt
2 pounds kielbasa, 12-inch link
½ cup grated cheese

In a large bowl, grate or mash potatoes, add 1 egg, flour, and salt, and mix thoroughly until a dough is formed. On a floured board, roll dough into rectangular shape (as a wrap for the kielbasa) to the thickness of a slice of bread. Place kielbasa on the long edge of the dough, and roll until dough is connected. Preheat oven to 350°F. In a small bowl, scramble remaining 1 egg and baste dough. Place on a cookie sheet and bake for 15 minutes. Remove from oven, and sprinkle cheese before serving.

MAKES 2 SERVINGS

DEEP-FRIED PORK CHOPS
(Vyprážaný Rezeň)

6 large pork chops
dash of garlic powder
salt and pepper to taste
2 tablespoons flour
2 eggs
1 cup bread crumbs
2 cups vegetable oil

Tenderize pork chops by beating with mallet. Sprinkle chops with garlic powder, and salt and pepper. Set up 3 medium bowls: flour in the first, beaten eggs in the second, and bread crumbs in the third. Cover the pork chops first with flour, then with egg, and finally with bread crumbs. Heat oil in medium skillet and deep-fry pork chops, taking care to fry both sides. Place on paper towels to drain excess oil. Serve with mixed rice and peas.

MAKES 6 SERVINGS

PORK CHOP SANDWICH
(Bravčový Sandvič)

4 large pork chops
salt and pepper to taste
1 stick (8 tablespoons) butter
4 eggs
4 pieces bread, sliced thick
1 large clove garlic

Tenderize pork chops by beating with mallet. Add salt and pepper to pork chops. Melt 4 tablespoons butter in large skillet and fry pork chops on both sides. In a small skillet, melt 1 tablespoon butter, and fry eggs (sunny side up). In another medium skillet, melt the remaining 3 tablespoons butter, and fry bread until golden brown. Scrape garlic clove across bread, place bread on plate, next place pork chop on bread, then add egg to bread, and serve.

MAKES 4 SERVINGS

PORK LOIN WITH SAUERKRAUT
(Bravčové S Kapustou)

2 pounds pork loin
4 cloves garlic
2 pounds sauerkraut
1 pouch powdered onion soup
4 mushrooms, sliced

Preheat oven to 350°F. Wash pork thoroughly, and place in baking dish. Make 4 cuts into meat, and stuff with garlic cloves. Add 2 cups water, and bake for 3 hours. In a large mixing bowl, mix sauerkraut with onion soup powder and mushrooms. Add to baking pan, and bake for 1 additional hour. Serve with baked potatoes.

MAKES 8 SERVINGS

PIEŠŤANY CUTLET
(Piešťanský Rezeň)

1 pound veal (sliced into 5 pieces)
3 eggs
¼ cup flour
½ cup milk
2 tablespoons raisins
dash of salt
1 cup vegetable oil

Tenderize veal by beating with mallet. In a large mixing bowl combine eggs, flour, milk, and raisins. Mix batter well. Salt veal slices, and dip into batter. Heat oil in large skillet, and deep-fry veal slices for 5 minutes or until golden brown. Serve with rice, potatoes, or dumplings (page 34).

MAKES 5 SERVINGS

SPIŠ MEAT DELICACY
(Spišská Pochúťka)

1 pound veal, sliced
2 tablespoons oil
1 large onion, chopped
salt and pepper to taste
1 teaspoon paprika
8 slices pepperoni
4 beef hot dogs, 1-inch sections
2 tomatoes, diced
2 tablespoons grated cheese

In a large pan, add veal and oil, and sauté for 10 minutes. Add onion, salt, pepper, paprika, pepperoni, hot dogs, 1 cup water, and tomatoes. Cook for 15 minutes. Place on serving dish, sprinkle with cheese, and serve.

MAKES 6 SERVINGS

VEAL RISSOTO
(Rizoto)

2 tablespoons oil
1 large onion, chopped fine
1½ pounds veal, cut into cubes
1 teaspoon salt
1 tablespoon paprika
dash of pepper
¾ cup cooked rice
1 cup canned peas

Add oil and onion to skillet, and brown. Add veal, and brown. Add salt, paprika, and pepper and stir well. Add 2 cups water and simmer for 45 minutes. Add peas and rice to meat, mix well and serve.

MAKES 4 SERVINGS

VEAL STEW WITH DUMPLINGS
(Telací Guláš s Knedlou)

½ cup oil
½ cup flour
1 pound veal, cut into cubes
½ cup diced carrots
½ cup diced potatoes
¼ cup chopped celery
¼ cup chopped onion
½ cup fresh peas
1 bay leaf
1 teaspoon Worcestershire sauce
1 8-ounce can tomato sauce
salt and pepper to taste

Heat oil in skillet. Place flour on large plate, and roll veal in flour until totally coated. Add to oil, and sauté until brown. Add 2 cups hot water, and cook for 1 hour. Add carrots, potatoes, celery, onion, peas, bay leaf, Worcestershire sauce, and cook for 30 minutes. Add tomato sauce and cook for additional 10 minutes.

DUMPLINGS:
1 cup flour
½ teaspoon salt
1½ teaspoons baking powder
½ cup milk
2 tablespoons vegetable oil

Bring a large pot of water to a boil. Mix flour, salt, baking powder, milk, and oil in large bowl to form soft dough. With a small spoon, drop into boiling water. Remove after 1 minute, or when dumplings float. (As an alternative, after goulash is finished, dumplings can be spooned directly into goulash and cooked for 1 minute.)

Combine veal with dumplings, add salt and pepper, and serve.

MAKES 6 SERVINGS

BEEF BIRDS
(Hovädzie Vtáčky)

1½ cups bread crumbs
¾ teaspoon salt
1½ teaspoons sage
1 tablespoon diced celery
1 tablespoon minced parsley
½ teaspoon pepper
5 tablespoons butter
¼ cup minced onions
6 steaks (3 × 5 × ¼ inch thick)
2 tablespoons flour
¼ cup oil
2 cups strained tomatoes
½ teaspoon horseradish

In a medium bowl, add bread crumbs, salt, sage, celery, parsley, and pepper and mix. In a large skillet, melt butter, add onions, and lightly sauté. Slowly add the bread crumb mixture to the butter and onions, continually stirring until the contents are golden brown. Add approximately ⅙ of the mixture to each steak, roll and tie with a string. In a separate container, blend the flour with 3 tablespoons water for later use. Heat oil in a heavy skillet, add steak rolls, and brown. Add tomatoes, cover and simmer for 1 hour. Remove the steaks from the skillet, add the flour and water mixture and simmer until thickening occurs. Ladle over steaks. Garnish with horseradish. Remove string, if desired, before serving.

MAKES 6 SERVINGS

BEEF ROULDER
(Mäsová Roláda)

1½ pounds thinly sliced round steak
2 hard-boiled egg yolks
2 sardines (can substitute fried bacon)
1 medium onion, chopped
2 tablespoons sour cream
dash of pepper
1 teaspoon salt
2 tablespoons oil
1 cup light cream
1 tablespoon flour

Preheat oven to 350°F. Tenderize steak with wooden mallet (both sides). Make a paste with the egg yolks and sardines. Add onion, sour cream, pepper, and salt to paste, and mix. Spoon paste onto steak, roll into cylindrical shape, and fasten with toothpicks, or tie with string. Heat oil in skillet, fry steak until uniformly brown. Place steak, pan drippings, and ½ cup water into covered dish, and bake for 1 hour. Combine light cream with flour and mix until uniform. Spoon mixture onto steak, and bake for an additional 10 minutes. Serve with noodles or rice.

MAKES 4 TO 6 SERVINGS

BEEF WITH SOUR CREAM AND MUSHROOMS
(Hovädzie s Smotanou a Hríbami)

1 pound ground beef
½ pound (2 cups) sliced mushrooms
1 tablespoon butter
1 tablespoon flour
1 cup sour cream
½ teaspoon salt
dash of pepper

Fry beef in skillet until brown, then drain excess oil. Add mushrooms to beef, and sauté for 2 minutes. In a separate pot, melt butter, add flour, and blend until flour is lightly browned. Add sour cream while stirring continuously. Pour meat and mushrooms into sauce, add salt and pepper, and cook for 4 minutes. Serve over cooked noodles.

MAKES 4 TO 6 SERVINGS

BEEF WITH VEGETABLES
(Hovädzie na Zelenine)

1 pound beef, sliced ¼-inch thick
1 tablespoon oil
1 onion, chopped
4 peppercorns
1 bay leaf
salt to taste
2 carrots, sliced
2 sprigs parsley
1 stalk celery, chopped
1 kohlrabi, chopped
2 green peppers, sliced
1 large tomato, sliced
1½ teaspoons flour

Wash beef and towel dry. Heat oil in a medium skillet, and brown beef on all sides. Add onion, peppercorns, and bay leaf to skillet, and sauté for 50 minutes, carefully adding up to 2 cups of water to prevent burning. Add salt, carrots, parsley, celery, kohlrabi, peppers, and tomato to skillet, and cook for an additional 15 minutes. Remove meat from skillet and put on a plate. Mash the contents of the skillet, and carefully sprinkle flour into the mixture. Return meat to the skillet and cook for 5 minutes. Serve with mashed potatoes, noodles, or pasta.

MAKES 6 SERVINGS

COUNTRY BEEF
(Hovädzie Nadivo)

1 pound prime beef
1 medium onion
2 cloves garlic
2 bay leaves
10 peppercorns
dash of salt
1 teaspoon vinegar
2 large carrots
1 sprig parsley
1 stalk celery
1 tablespoon flour
½ cup sour cream
½ teaspoon sugar
1 teaspoon mustard

Wash beef and place in large pot with 2 quarts water, onion, garlic, bay leaves, peppercorns, salt, and vinegar. Place in refrigerator and let stand overnight. On the second day, add carrots, parsley, and celery, and cook for 2 hours, or until beef is tender. Remove beef and cut into ½-inch slices. Strain liquid into another pot. Remove peppercorns and bay leaves and discard. Mash remaining ingredients through colander, and discard residue. Place meat and mashed ingredients into pot with liquid. Mix flour into sour cream, and add to pot. Add sugar and mustard, and cook for 5 minutes. Serve with dark bread, or pasta.

MAKES 4 SERVINGS

SOUR BEEF
(Mäso Na Kyslo)

2 medium carrots, chopped
2 medium onions, minced
1 cup vegetable oil
1 small clove garlic, minced
1 shallot, minced
6 whole peppercorns
½ cup chopped celery
2 cups vinegar
2 cups white wine
½ cup brown sugar
1 tablespoon salt
2 pounds bottom round prime beef
2 cups red wine
1 cup tomato paste
1 cup beef stock
1 cup sour cream
juice of 1 lemon

Brown carrots and onions in 2 tablespoons oil in large pot. Add remaining oil, garlic, shallot, peppercorns, and celery and simmer for 3 minutes. Add vinegar, white wine, 2 cups water, sugar, and salt, mix and let cool. Add beef, and marinate in refrigerator overnight. Cook on stove until juice is reduced by half. Add red wine, tomato paste, and beef stock and cook for 2 hours. Add sour cream and lemon juice, and serve with dumplings (page 34) or pasta.

MAKES 6 TO 8 SERVINGS

MEAT BALLS
(Fašírky)

1 pound ground beef
1 cup evaporated canned milk
1 cup grated carrots
½ cup bread crumbs
1 small onion, grated
2 small cloves garlic, chopped
salt and pepper to taste
4 tablespoons oil
1 can (10.5 ounces) cream of
    mushroom soup
1 cup uncooked rice

Preheat oven to 350°F. In a large bowl add beef, milk, carrots, bread crumbs, onion, garlic, salt, and pepper. Mix well, and shape into small balls. Heat oil in skillet, add meat balls, and uniformly brown. Remove meat balls from skillet and place in casserole dish. Mix mushroom soup with 1 cup water, and add to casserole dish. Bake for 25 minutes. Add rice to 2 cups water, bring to a boil, reduce heat to simmer, cover, and cook for 20 minutes. Serve meat balls with rice.

MAKES 4 TO 6 SERVINGS

SLOVAK MEAT LOAF
(Fašírka)

2 pounds ground beef
½ teaspoon garlic powder
salt and pepper to taste
2 eggs
½ pouch powdered onion soup
1 tablespoon oatmeal
2 cups bread crumbs

Preheat oven to 350°F. In a large mixing bowl add beef, garlic powder, salt and pepper, eggs, onion soup, and oatmeal. Mix thoroughly by hand. Shape meat into loaf. Pour bread crumbs on large plate, and coat meat loaf on all sides. Pour any leftover bread crumbs on top of meat loaf. Place in loaf pan and bake for 1 hour. Serve with mash potatoes, baked potatoes, potato salad, or rice.

MAKES 8 SERVINGS

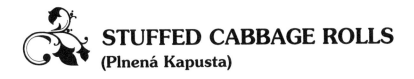

STUFFED CABBAGE ROLLS
(Plnená Kapusta)

1 large head cabbage
1 cup shredded cabbage
¾ cup uncooked rice
½ cup diced onions
¼ cup diced green pepper
¼ cup diced carrots
1 pound ground beef
¾ teaspoon salt
½ teaspoon pepper
½ cup sour cream
½ cup canned tomato soup

Preheat oven to 350°F. Steam head of cabbage for 15 minutes, separate leaves, and set aside. Mix shredded cabbage, rice, onions, peppers, carrots, beef, salt, and pepper. Form this material into loose rolls, and wrap in cabbage leaf. Place rolls into greased casserole, and pour 2 cups water over rolls. Bake for 1½ hours. Stir sour cream and tomato soup together, pour over the cabbage rolls, reduce heat to 300°F, and bake an additional 30 minutes. Serve hot.

MAKES 6 TO 8 SERVINGS

STUFFED PEPPERS
(Plnené Papriky)

10 medium green bell peppers
1 onion, chopped fine
1 tablespoon butter
½ pound ground beef
½ pound ground pork
½ cup cooked rice
1 egg
salt and pepper
1 cup diced canned tomatoes
¼ cup flour
1 cup sour cream

Wash peppers and remove caps, carefully coring the shell. Fry onion in butter until brown. Mix beef and pork with onion, rice, egg, salt, and pepper. Stuff into peppers and place in large pot. Pour tomatoes over peppers. Add salt and pepper to taste. Fill pot with 2 cups water, cover, simmer slowly for 1 hour. Temporarily remove peppers from pot. Mix flour with ¼ cup sour cream. Add to the pot, stir well, and bring to a boil. Add the remaining ¾ cup sour cream, replace the stuffed peppers, and boil for an additional 10 minutes. Serve as is, or with bread or mashed potatoes.

MAKES 10 SERVINGS

BROILED LIVER
(Grilovaná Pečienka)

1 pound sliced liver
2 cups milk
1 cup bread crumbs
1 tablespoon butter

In a large bowl, soak liver in milk for 4 hours in refrigerator. Remove liver and pat dry with paper towel. Spread bread crumbs on a flat plate, and coat liver completely with crumbs. Use ½ tablespoon of the butter to coat one side of the liver. Place liver on oven broiler grate. Broil until brown. Turn liver over, coat with remaining ½ tablespoon butter, and broil until brown. Serve immediately to ensure tenderness.

MAKES 4 SERVINGS

FRIED LIVER
(Vyprážaná Pečeň)

¼ cup flour
2 eggs
1 cup bread crumbs
½ pound calves liver, thinly sliced
2 cups vegetable oil

Prepare 3 bowls: add flour to the first bowl, thoroughly beat eggs in the second bowl, and add bread crumbs to the third bowl. Take liver, one slice at a time, coat with flour from the first bowl, coat with eggs from the second bowl, and finally, coat with bread crumbs from the third bowl. Heat oil in a large skillet and fry liver and both sides until golden brown. Serve immediately to prevent hardening. Serve with french fries, mashed potatoes, or potato salad.

MAKES 4 SERVINGS

GOULASH
(Guláš)

2 tablespoons oil
3 cups sliced onions
½ pound beef, cut into cubes
½ pound pork, cut into cubes
½ pound veal, cut into cubes
½ green pepper, chopped
2 tablespoons paprika
1 teaspoon salt

Heat oil in heavy skillet. Add onions and fry until lightly
browned. Add beef, pork, veal, pepper, paprika, salt and
1 quart water, and simmer for 1 hour or until meat is tender.
Serve with rye bread.

MAKES 6 SERVINGS

SAUERKRAUT GOULASH
(Kapustný Guláš)

1 pound sauerkraut
2 pounds spareribs
2 tablespoons butter
1 medium onion, chopped
2 tablespoons flour
1 teaspoon salt
1 teaspoon paprika
½ cup sour cream

Cook sauerkraut and spareribs with 2 cups water in large pot for 1 hour. Melt butter in small skillet, add onion, flour, and salt, and mix until brown. Add to sauerkraut, and cook for 10 minutes. Add paprika, mix, and remove from heat. Add sour cream, mix, and serve.

MAKES 4 TO 6 SERVINGS

FISH PATTIES
(Rybacie Karbonátky)

2 cups vegetable oil
2 pounds fish, cubed
½ cup milk
4 buns, cubed
1 small onion, diced
salt and pepper to taste
1 egg
2 egg yolks
1 cup bread crumbs
1 cup grated cheese

In a large skillet, add 2 tablespoons oil and fish, and sauté for 8 minutes. In a large mixing bowl, add milk, buns, onion, salt, pepper, egg, and egg yolks, and mix thoroughly. Add fish to mixing bowl and mix thoroughly. Pour bread crumbs on large plate. Form patties from mixture, and coat with bread crumbs. In large skillet, add remaining oil and bring to boil, then fry patties until golden brown. Place patties on paper towel to absorb excess oil. Sprinkle cheese on patties while hot. Serve with mashed potatoes.

MAKES 6 SERVINGS

FISH RAGU
(Rybacie Ragú)

2 pounds fish, washed, filleted and cubed
dash of salt
1 stick (8 tablespoons) butter
1 cup mushrooms, diced
1 cup white wine
1 cup sour cream
1 tablespoon flour
2 egg yolks
juice of 1 lemon
dash of pepper

Preheat oven to 350°F. In a large skillet, add fish, salt, and
6 tablespoons butter, and sauté for 8 minutes (until fish is soft).
In another large skillet, add remaining 2 tablespoons butter
and mushrooms, and sauté until golden brown. Add wine to
mushrooms, and set aside. In a large bowl, thoroughly mix
sour cream with flour. Add egg yolks, lemon juice, and pepper
to sour cream, and mix. Add mushrooms to mixing bowl.
Place fish in baking pan, cover with contents of mixing bowl,
and bake for 20 minutes. Serve with rice or macaroni.

MAKES 4 SERVINGS

MARINATED FISH
(Marinovaná Ryba)

2 pounds fish, filleted
1 stick (8 tablespoons) butter
1 cup vinegar
8 peppercorns
2 bay leaves
dash of salt
1 small onion, chopped

Preheat oven to 350°F. Wash fish, place in pan, add 1 table-spoon butter, and bake in oven for 20 minutes. In a large pot, add 1 quart water, vinegar, peppercorns, bay leaves, salt, and onion, and cook for 5 minutes. Pour contents over fish in pan, let cool, and refrigerate overnight. Remove fish and place on large serving plate, and discard other contents of pan. Melt remaining 7 tablespoons butter, pour over fish, and serve with salad and bread.

MAKES 6 SERVINGS

Desserts
&
Breads

APPLE FRITTERS
(Jablká V Župane)

1 egg
⅓ cup milk
1 cup all-purpose flour
1½ teaspoons baking powder
3 tablespoons sugar
¼ teaspoon salt
1 cup apple slices, ¼ inch thick
oil
powdered sugar

Mix egg and milk in a large bowl. In another bowl, sift flour, add baking powder, sugar, salt, and sift again. Combine with egg and milk, and stir in apple slices. In a large skillet, heat oil to 370°F. Spoon fritters into oil and fry until golden brown. Place on absorbent paper to drain excess oil. Sprinkle with powdered sugar and serve.

MAKES 4 SERVINGS

APPLE STRUDEL
(Jablková Štrudla)

2½ cups flour
2 eggs, slightly beaten
1¼ teaspoons salt
2 tablespoons butter, melted

FILLING:
5 cups sliced apples, ⅛ inch thick
1 cup sugar
½ cup raisins
1 cup chopped walnuts
1 teaspoon cinnamon
½ cup bread crumbs or graham cracker crumbs
6 tablespoons butter, melted

In a large bowl, sift flour, and mix in eggs, ½ cup warm water, salt and butter. Stir until thoroughly blended. Sprinkle flour on board and then knead dough until uniform and shiny. (It is important to make sure the ingredients are completely mixed so that the dough stretches without tearing). Cover with warm bowl and allow to stand undisturbed in a warm place for about 20 minutes.

Prepare filling by mixing apples with sugar, raisins, nuts, cinnamon, bread crumbs, and butter.

Preheat oven to 450°F. Cover table with white, lint-free cloth, and secure to table. Flour cloth well. Place dough in center of cloth and walk around table while carefully pulling and stretching dough into rectangular shape. Ideally, the dough is made as thin as tissue paper. Spread the filling uniformly over the dough. Fold opposite edges in ½ inch. Roll from unfolded edge. (Roll may be started by slightly raising cloth). Carefully place roll onto buttered cookie sheet. Bake 10 minutes. Lower heat to 350°F and bake for 30 more minutes. Remove from oven and let cool. Make slices about 1 inch wide.

MAKES 10 SERVINGS

DELICATE APPLE CAKE
(Krehký Jablčník)

1¾ cups flour
1½ teaspoon baking powder
3 egg yolks
1 stick (½ cup) butter
2 tablespoons sugar

FILLING:
6 apples, diced
½ cup sugar
¾ cup chopped nuts
¾ cup raisins
1 tablespoon cinnamon
Pam (spray shortening)

Preheat oven to 350°F. In a large mixing bowl, add flour and
baking powder and mix. Add egg yolks, butter, 3 tablespoons
cold water, and sugar, and work into a dough. Divide dough
into 2 equal parts. Place one part dough on a floured board
and roll until ¼ inch thick. Repeat with other piece of dough.
Mix filling ingredients together. Spray Pam on pie pan, place
1 piece dough on pan, add filling, cover with other piece of
dough. Pinch edges together, make air holes in dough with
fork, and bake for 40 minutes.

MAKES 8 SERVINGS

DOBOSH TORTE
(Dobošová Torta)

6 eggs
1 cup powdered sugar
1 cup flour

FILLING:
1 cup milk
1 cup powdered sugar
½ cup cocoa
2 egg yolks
1 tablespoon cornstarch
1 tablespoon vanilla
1 pound (2 cups) butter
2 tablespoons chopped almonds

Preheat oven to 325˚F. Separate egg yolks from whites. In
a medium mixing bowl, combine egg yolks with 1 cup sugar.
In another mixing bowl, beat egg whites until consistency of
whipped cream. Slowly mix flour into whipped egg whites
to prevent lumps. Now, slowly add the egg whites/flour mix
to the egg yolk/sugar mix. Pour contents into six small
cookie sheets (layers are to be about ¼ inch thick). Bake for
10 minutes. Set pans aside to cool. While cakes are cooling,
prepare filling as follows: In a small pan, add ½ cup milk and
1 cup sugar, boil for 2 minutes and set aside. In medium bowl,
add ½ cup cold milk, and mix with cocoa, egg yolks, cornstarch,

and vanilla. Add cooled milk mixture to bowl, and mix. Melt butter in small pan, add to bowl, and mix thoroughly. To finish the cake, cover each layer with filling and stack layers. Sprinkle almonds on top layer.

MAKES 12 SERVINGS

WALNUT TORTE
(Orechová Torta)

10 eggs
2 cups powdered sugar
1 cup finely ground walnuts
Pam (spray shortening)

FILLING:
2 sticks (1 cup) butter
2 cups powdered sugar
2 egg yolks
1 egg
1 teaspoon vanilla

Preheat oven to 350°F. Separate egg yolks from whites. In a large bowl, add 10 egg yolks and sugar, and beat until foamy. In another large bowl, beat egg whites until consistency of whipped cream. Fold yolk mixture into egg whites. Gradually fold in walnuts. Pour mix into 3 greased, 8-inch round cake pans, and bake for 1 hour. Let cool to room temperature before applying filling.

To make filling, in a large mixing bowl, add butter, sugar, and egg yolks. Mix and slowly add egg and vanilla. Mix thoroughly, until filling is smooth. Spread between layers, on top layer, and on sides. Ready to serve (needs refrigeration).

MAKES 12 PIECES

CHESTNUT PUREE
(Gaštanové Pyré)

2 pounds chestnuts
4 cups milk
1 cup sugar
2 tablespoons vanilla
1 tablespoon rum

Peel chestnuts (cut chestnut skin with knife, and peel with fingers), cut chestnuts in half, add to a pot with milk, and cook for 20 minutes. Using a potato masher, mash chestnuts thoroughly, then add sugar, vanilla, and rum, and mix. Let cool, spoon into cocktail glasses, and serve.

MAKES 8 SERVINGS

FANKY
(Čeregy)

2 cups flour
½ teaspoon salt
2 tablespoons sugar
1 tablespoon butter
5 egg yolks
2 tablespoons sour cream
2 tablespoons wine or beer
oil
powdered sugar

Sift flour in bowl and mix in salt, sugar, and butter. Beat egg yolks and pour into bowl. Add sour cream and wine. Mix until blended well. Place dough on floured board and knead until uniform. Divide into 2 or 3 pieces, and roll into very thin sheets. Cut into about 5-inch diamond-shaped pieces. Next, cut a 2-inch slit lengthwise in the diamond, and pull one end through to shape them. Fry in pan (one-layer deep) in very hot oil until golden brown (about 1 to 2 minutes). Place on absorbent paper to drain excess oil, and dust with powdered sugar.

MAKES 8 SERVINGS

FRUIT CAKE
(Ovocné Koláče)

3½ cups flour
1 stick (½ cup) butter
2 egg yolks
1 package dry yeast
2 tablespoons sugar
dash of salt
grated peel of 1 lemon
½ cup warm milk
Pam (spray shortening)
6 apples or 10 plums or 10 apricots or
      2 cups blueberries

In a large mixing bowl add flour, butter, egg yolks, yeast, sugar, salt, lemon peel, and milk. Thoroughly mix with hands and place in warm, draft-free spot for 4 hours. Place raised dough on floured board, and gently roll dough into rectangle (approximately 12 inches by 16 inches). Spray Pam on baking pan, and place dough in pan. Preheat oven to 350°F. Cut fruit into dice-size pieces and place on surface of dough. Bake for 50 minutes.

MAKES 16 SERVINGS

HONEY COOKIES
(Medovníky)

½ stick (4 tablespoons) butter
1 cup sugar
3 eggs
3 tablespoons honey
½ teaspoon cinnamon
½ teaspoon allspice
5 cups flour
1 teaspoon baking soda

Preheat oven to 325°F. In a large bowl, mix butter and sugar. Add eggs and honey, and mix thoroughly. In another large bowl, add cinnamon, allspice, flour, and baking soda, and mix thoroughly. Combine the contents of both bowls and mix until a smooth dough is formed. Roll dough on a floured board to a ¼ inch thickness. Use cookie cutters as desired. Place on greased cookie sheet and bake for 12 minutes.

MAKES APPROXIMATELY 24 COOKIES

JAM CRISSCROSS COOKIES
(Ovocné Kekse)

3 tablespoons whipping cream (liquid)
2 cups flour
2 sticks (1 cup) butter
1¼ cups sugar
2 eggs
1 teaspoon vanilla
1 teaspoon baking powder
1 pound jam

Preheat oven to 350°F. In a large bowl, add whipping cream, flour, butter, sugar, eggs, vanilla, and baking powder, and mix thoroughly to form a uniform dough. Take ¾ of the dough, and roll on a floured board to a rectangular shape to fit a 10-inch by 15-inch pan. (Refrigerate the remaining dough for 15 minutes.) Place dough into pan, and cover with jam. Remove dough from refrigerator, and roll into approximately 12 long strips, and crisscross diagonally across the jam. Bake for 25 minutes.

MAKES 16 SERVINGS

POPPY SEED COOKIES
(Makové Kekse)

2½ cups flour
dash of salt
½ teaspoon baking soda
¾ cup sugar
1 egg
½ cup sour cream
½ cup oil
1 teaspoon vanilla
¼ cup poppy seeds

Preheat oven to 375°F. In a large bowl, add flour, salt, baking soda, and sugar, and mix well. Add egg, sour cream, oil, vanilla, and poppy seeds, and mix until dough is uniform. Roll dough on a floured board to a thickness of ¼ inch. Cut (or form) into desired shapes with cookie cutters, place on greased, cookie sheet, and bake for 15 minutes.

MAKES APPROXIMATELY 24 COOKIES

WALNUT COOKIES
(Orechové Kekse)

4 sticks (1 pound) butter
½ pound (2 cups) ground walnuts
¼ cup powdered sugar
3 egg yolks
¼ cup milk
2 cups flour

Preheat oven to 350°F. In a large bowl, add butter, walnuts, sugar, and egg yolks, and mix well. Add milk and flour, and mix until dough is thick enough to roll. Roll dough on a floured board to a ¼ inch thickness. Use cookie cutters as desired. Place cookies on ungreased cookie sheet and bake for 20 minutes.

MAKES APPROXIMATELY 24 COOKIES

JELLY CAKES
(Lekvarove Koláčky)

FILLING:
8 egg whites
2½ pounds (7½ cups) chopped nuts
    (or jam/poppy seeds/apricots)
4 cups powdered sugar
1 teaspoon vanilla
1 tablespoon cinnamon
¾ cup warm milk

1 large cake yeast (or 1 envelope)
¼ cup warm milk
1 tablespoon baking powder
8 cups flour
4 sticks (1 pound) butter
1 pound (2 cups) shortening
1 pint sour cream
8 egg yolks

Combine all filling ingredients (except 1 egg white) in a bowl and mix well.

Mix yeast with milk. In large bowl, sift baking powder and flour, then add butter and shortening, and mix into dough. Add sour cream, beaten egg yolks, and milk with yeast. Mix dough until all lumps are gone, and place in refrigerator overnight. Preheat oven to 325°F. Take a portion and roll on floured board. Roll dough flat to about ¼ inch thick, and place generous amounts of filling in center. Then form into roll. Beat remaining egg white and brush on top and bake on ungreased cookie sheet for about 15 minutes. (Can also cut flattened dough into 3-inch squares, add filling, and fold corners into middle, or make into rolls).

MAKES 20 SERVINGS

KAVA CAKE
(Kávová Torta)

6 eggs
2 cups powdered sugar
6 tablespoons very strong prepared coffee
1 stick (8 tablespoons) butter, melted
1¾ cups flour
¼ teaspoon baking powder

FILLING:
1 cup milk
2 tablespoons finely ground coffee
1 cup powdered sugar
1 tablespoon cornstarch
2 egg yolks
1 tablespoon vanilla
2 sticks (1 cup) butter, melted
2 tablespoons rum

Preheat oven to 350°F. Separate egg yolks from egg whites.
In a large mixing bowl, add egg yolks and powdered sugar
and mix thoroughly. While mixing, slowly add coffee, and
butter. In another mixing bowl, add the egg whites and beat
until the consistency of whipped cream. In a third mixing bowl,
mix flour and baking powder, and slowly fold into the egg
whites. Take this bowl, and slowly fold into the bowl of egg
yolks. Pour contents into 2 8-inch round, greased cake pans
and bake for 40 minutes. After cakes have cooled, remove

from pans and place on plate. While cakes are cooling, prepare filling as follows: Boil milk and coffee grounds in a small pot for 5 minutes. Strain milk and dispose of coffee. Add sugar to milk and boil for 4 minutes and set aside to cool. In a small mixing bowl, mix cornstarch, egg yolks, and vanilla, and add to milk solution after it has cooled. Add butter and rum and let cool. Spread filling on each cake and stack cake.

MAKES 8 SERVINGS

MARZIPAN
(Marcipán)

2 cups powdered sugar
½ pound almonds, shelled and chopped fine
1 tablespoon water

In a mixing bowl, add sugar, almonds, and water, and work into a smooth dough. Place in refrigerator for one day. On a large plate, shape dough into small balls, or any shapes desired, and serve.

MAKES 24 PIECES

NUT ROLL
(Orechovník)

FILLING:
4 cups finely ground nuts (poppy seeds
    can be substituted)
2 cups milk
½ cup sugar

In a large pot, add nuts, milk, and sugar, and cook for
20 minutes. When cool, the filling is ready to use.

1 cake yeast (or 1 envelope)
1 cup warm milk
¼ cup sugar
9 cups sifted flour
8 eggs
2 sticks (½ cup) soft butter
2 teaspoons salt
2 tablespoons shortening
2 cups heavy cream
1 teaspoon vanilla

Mix yeast, milk, sugar, and 2 cups of flour in large bowl, and
set in warm place for 30 minutes. Separate eggs. Add beaten
egg yolks, butter, salt, shortening, and cream. Stir until all
lumps are gone. Beat egg whites until firm, add vanilla, and

add to bowl. Mix well, and slowly add 7 cups of flour. Knead until dough is free of lumps and elastic. Cover with dish towel and set aside in a warm spot until dough rises to double size (about 1 hour). Mix dough and allow to rise again for about ½ hour. Repeat this process two more times so that dough becomes light. Preheat oven to 350°F. Divide dough into 6 sections on lightly floured board. Roll until about ¼ inch thick, and spread with nut filling. Bake for about 45 minutes.

MAKES 20 SERVINGS

PANCAKES WITH COTTAGE CHEESE
(Palacinky So Syrom)

cooking oil
2 cups flour
½ cup milk
1 egg
pinch of salt
grated peel of ½ lemon

FILLING:
1 cup dry curd cottage cheese
3 tablespoons sugar
1 tablespoon raisins

Heat a few drops of oil in a nonstick frying pan. Combine flour, milk, ½ cup water, egg, salt, and lemon peel to form a batter. Ladle batter into hot pan, tilting the pan in a circular motion until batter thinly covers the pan. Cook for 1 to 2 minutes on medium heat, then turn over and cook another 30 seconds.

Mix all filling ingredients, spread on pancakes, and roll into finger shapes.

MAKES 6 TO 8 MEDIUM PANCAKES

PLUM TARTS
(Slivkové Knedličky)

8 medium potatoes
1 egg yolk
1 tablespoon butter
6 tablespoons flour
10 plums, pits removed
4 tablespoons ground poppy seeds
1 tablespoon powdered sugar

In 2 quarts water, boil potatoes until cooked. Peel and mash potatoes, add egg yolk and butter, and mix thoroughly. Add flour, and knead until dough has uniform consistency. Roll dough on a flat board until ⅛ inch thick. Cut dough into 2-inch by 2-inch squares, place plum in center, and fold dough over plum until completely covered. Pinch edges closed. In another pot, bring 2 quarts water to boil, add plum tarts, and boil for 6 minutes (or until tarts float). Remove from water, place on serving tray, sprinkle with poppy seeds and sugar.

MAKES 4 SERVINGS

POPPY SEED CAKE
(Makový Koláč)

1 cup shortening
1 cup sugar
4 eggs
½ pound poppy seeds
1 teaspoon baking soda
2 cups flour
1 cup sour cream
1 teaspoon vanilla

Preheat oven to 350°F. In a large bowl, add shortening and sugar, and mix well. Separate egg yolks from whites. Add poppy seeds, egg yolks, baking soda, flour, sour cream, vanilla, and again, mix well. In a small bowl, beat the egg whites until the consistency of whipped cream. Slowly fold contents into first bowl. Pour batter into Bundt cake pan and bake for 50 minutes.

MAKES 12 SLICES

POPPY SEED DUMPLINGS
(Makové Buchty)

3½ cups flour
dash of salt
3 egg yolks
2 tablespoons sugar, plus additional
    for sprinkling
2 packages dry yeast
½ cup warm milk
1 stick (½ cup) butter
Pam (spray shortening)

FILLING:

Poppy seed
1 cup ground poppy seeds
1 tablespoon sugar
grated peel of ½ lemon
1 teaspoon vanilla

Add all ingredients with ½ cup water in a small pan, and
cook for 10 minutes. Let cool before stuffing dumpling.

In a large mixing bowl, add flour, salt, egg yolks, sugar, yeast,
and milk. Work into a dough. Melt butter, let cool, then add
to dough. Thoroughly work dough, then let sit (in bowl) for
1 hour. Place dough on floured board and gently roll to ½ inch
thick. Cut into 1-inch by 2-inch pieces, place filling on dough,
fold dough over into 1-inch square and pinch edges shut.

Preheat oven to 350°F, spray large cookie sheet with Pam, and place dumplings on sheet about 1-inch apart, and bake for 25 minutes. Remove from oven, sprinkle with sugar, and serve.

MAKES 12 SERVINGS

PRUNE CAKE
(Slivkový Koláč)

2 sticks (1 cup) butter
1 cup sugar
2 eggs
1½ cups flour
1 teaspoon baking soda
½ cup sour cream
1 cup sliced cooked prunes
1 teaspoon vanilla
½ teaspoon ground cloves
1 teaspoon cinnamon
½ teaspoon nutmeg

Preheat oven to 350°F. In a large bowl, mix butter with sugar. Add eggs and mix again. In a small bowl, sift flour and baking soda, and add to first bowl. Add sour cream, prunes, vanilla, cloves, cinnamon, and nutmeg, and mix thoroughly. Pour mix into a 9-inch by 12-inch, greased pan, and bake for 30 minutes.

MAKES 12 SLICES

PUNCH CAKE
(Punčová Torta)

12 eggs
2 cups powdered sugar
1¾ cups all-purpose flour
1 tablespoon cocoa
1 tablespoon tart jam

FILLING:
1 cup white wine
½ cup rum
2 tablespoons orange marmalade
1 stick (½ cup) butter, melted
juice of 1 lemon
grated peel of ½ orange
2 tablespoons vanilla

Preheat oven to 350°F. Separate egg yolks from whites and place yolks in one mixing bowl, and whites in another mixing bowl. Add sugar to egg yolks and mix until foamy. Beat the egg whites thoroughly. Into the egg whites, slowly add flour while gently mixing. Now slowly combine the egg mixtures, while gently mixing until a thin dough forms. Pour dough into 3 bowls. Add cocoa to one bowl. Add marmalade to a second bowl. Pour the contents of the 3 bowls into separate 8-inch, greased cake pans, and bake for 20 minutes.

While cakes are cooling, prepare filling as follows: Combine wine, rum, orange marmalade, butter, lemon juice, orange peel, and vanilla, and thoroughly mix. After cake has cooled, stack the layers, after first pouring the filling over each layer. Place in refrigerator for 6 hours before serving.

MAKES 12 SERVINGS

VANILLA WAFER CAKE
(Vanilova Torta)

1 cup prepared coffee
1 tablespoon rum
8 cups vanilla wafers
2 tablespoons tart jam
¾ cup milk
1 cup chopped nuts
8 ounces whipping cream

Mix coffee and rum in a small bowl. Dip wafers into coffee/rum mix, and arrange one layer on bottom of 7-inch by 10-inch baking pan. Cover wafers with jam. Prepare another layer of wafers by dipping in the coffee/rum mix and placing on top of jam. In a small pot, boil milk and nuts for 10 minutes. Let cool, then spoon onto wafers. Cover with third layer of dipped wafers, and place in refrigerator overnight. Before serving, whip the cream and pour over wafers. Cut into small squares and serve.

MAKES 12 SERVINGS

RICE PUDDING
(Ryžový Nákyp)

1 pound (2½ cups) white rice
2 cups milk
dash of salt
3 tablespoons sugar
4 eggs
½ cup raisins
1 tablespoon vanilla
½ cup chopped nuts
Pam (spray shortening)
4 apples, peeled and sliced
syrup

Cook rice in milk for 45 minutes. During cooking, add salt and 2 tablespoons sugar. Preheat oven to 350°F. Separate egg whites from yolks. To the egg whites, add 1 tablespoon sugar, and whip until foamy. When rice is cooked, add egg yolks, raisins, vanilla, nuts, and egg whites. Take a 7-inch by 10-inch baking dish, spray with Pam, pour ½ of the rice mixture into the dish, place apple slices on top of rice, and pour remaining rice on top of apples. Place in oven and bake for 20 minutes. Serve with syrup.

MAKES 4 SERVINGS

SLOVAK DONUTS
(Šišky)

3½ cups flour
dash of salt
3 large egg yolks
½ stick (4 tablespoons) butter, melted
1 tablespoon powdered sugar
1 tablespoon rum
1 package dry yeast
2 cups warm milk
4 cups vegetable oil
2 tablespoons granulated sugar

In a large mixing bowl, add flour, salt, egg yolks, butter, powdered sugar, rum, yeast, and milk, and work into dough. Cover bowl with a cloth, place in a warm, draft-free place, and let sit for an hour. Remove dough and place on floured board, and gently roll dough into flat layer about ½ inch thick. Take a small glass (diameter of about 2 inches), dip rim in flour, and pressure cut the dough. Let dough sit for 20 minutes to rise. Heat oil in large skillet and fry donuts on both sides until golden brown. Remove from oil and place on absorbent paper to remove excess oil, and to cool. Place on plate, sprinkle with granulated sugar, and serve.

MAKES 4 SERVINGS

COTTAGE CHEESE BREAD CAKE
(Tvarohová Žemľovka)

1 teaspoon butter
1 cup milk
8 slices white bread
1 cup cottage cheese
2 egg yolks
2 tablespoons powered sugar
1 teaspoon vanilla
1 teaspoon lemon juice
1 tablespoon raisins
1 egg
dash of cinnamon
syrup

Preheat oven to 350°F. Apply butter to baking dish. Add milk to large bowl. Individually, dip 4 bread slices in milk, and place in baking dish. Use a cheesecloth to remove excess liquid from cottage cheese. In a separate bowl, add egg yolk, dry cottage cheese, powdered sugar, vanilla, lemon juice, and raisins, mix thoroughly, and spoon onto bread. Dip the remaining pieces of bread into the milk and place over the mix. Add egg and cinnamon to remaining milk, mix thoroughly, and pour over bread. Bake for 30 minutes. Serve with syrup.

MAKES 4 SERVINGS

COTTAGE CHEESE DOUGH BALLS
(Tvarohové Knedličky)

8 ounces cottage cheese
2 tablespoons butter
1 egg
2 tablespoons powdered sugar
1 cup flour
½ stick (4 tablespoons) butter
1 cup bread crumbs

Use cheesecloth to remove excess liquid from cheese. In a large mixing bowl, add dry cheese, butter, egg, sugar, and flour, and knead until thoroughly mixed. In a separate pot, bring 2 quarts water with ½ teaspoon salt to boil. With your hands, form 1-inch-diameter balls from the mix, and drop into boiling water. After all balls have thoroughly cooked (they are floating on the surface), pour contents into colander. In a small skillet, melt butter, and add bread crumbs. Sauté until crispy brown, and pour over cheese balls.

MAKES 4 SERVINGS

COTTAGE CHEESE DUMPLINGS
(Syrove Buchty)

3½ cups flour
dash of salt
3 egg yolks
2 tablespoons sugar, plus additional for sprinkling
2 packages dry yeast
½ cup warm milk
1 stick (½ cup) butter
Pam (spray shortening)

FILLING:

Cottage Cheese
8 ounces cottage cheese
1 tablespoon sugar
grated peel of ½ lemon
1 egg yolk
dash of cinnamon
Thoroughly mix all ingredients.

In a large mixing bowl, add flour, salt, egg yolks, sugar, yeast, and milk. Work into a dough. Melt butter, let cool, then add to dough. Thoroughly work dough, then let sit (in bowl) for 1 hour. Place dough on floured board and gently roll to ½ inch thick. Cut into 1-inch by 2-inch pieces, place filling on dough, fold dough over into 1-inch square and pinch edges shut. Preheat oven to 350°F, spray large cookie sheet with Pam, and place dumplings on sheet about 1-inch apart, and bake for 25 minutes. Remove from oven, sprinkle with sugar, and serve.

MAKES 12 SERVINGS

BRAIDED BREAD
(Bábovka)

1 cake yeast (or 1 envelope)
2 teaspoons sugar
1 cup boiled milk
6 cups flour
1 can (12 ounces) evaporated milk
1 tablespoon butter, melted, plus additional
    for topping
2 egg yolks, beaten
¾ teaspoon salt

In a large bowl, dissolve yeast and sugar in warm milk, add sifted flour, and mix. Set in warm place and allow to rise for 10 minutes. Add warmed evaporated milk, 1 cup warm water, butter, egg yolks, and salt. Knead thoroughly, cover, and set in warm place free of draft. Let dough rise for 2 hours. Separate dough into 3 portions. With your hands, form each piece into a rope-like shape, approximately 12 inches long by 1 inch diameter. Cover and let stand for 15 minutes. Braid, place in buttered pans. Allow to rise until doubled in bulk, for about 30 minutes. Preheat over to 350˚F. Brush with melted butter. Bake for 10 minutes, then raise temperature to 375˚F, and bake for 1 hour.

MAKES 20 SERVINGS

CHRISTMAS DUMPLINGS
(Bobálky)

1 recipe Braided Bread (Bábovka), (page 128)

1½ cups ground poppy seeds
3 cups milk
1 cup sugar

Prepare *bábovka* as directed up to the braiding step. Do not separate into 3 portions. Instead, pinch off portion of dough, roll out on floured board by hand to make roll about ½ inch in diameter. Place on cookie sheet. Cut with edge of teaspoon into bite-size pieces. Preheat oven to 375°F. Let rise for 10 minutes. Bake for 15 minutes, or until lightly brown. When cool, separate, and place in colander. Pour boiling water over bobálky. Drain any excess water.

Cook poppy seed in ¾ cup water for 10 minutes. Boil milk, add sugar (according to taste), pour over poppy seed and mix. Add to bobálky. Mix well and serve immediately.

MAKES 20 SERVINGS

EASTER BREAD
(Paska)

1 cake yeast or 1 envelope
1 cup boiling milk
1 stick (½ cup) butter
1 teaspoon salt
3 cups flour

In a small bowl, crumble yeast into 2 tablespoons lukewarm water, and let stand for 5 minutes. In a large bowl, pour milk over butter and salt, and cool to lukewarm. Add yeast mixture, and 1½ cups flour, and mix until smooth. Add remaining 1½ cups flour and knead until smooth. Let rise until dough doubles in bulk, about 1 hour. Divide dough into 2 equal parts. Preheat over to 375˚F. Place dough in greased bread pans and bake for 1 hour.

MAKES 2 LOAVES

STUFFED BREAD
(Plnený Chlieb)

1 loaf Italian Bread, unsliced
½ cup milk
½ cup sour cream
4 hard-boiled eggs, cubed
2 cups baked ham, cubed
½ stick (4 tablespoons) butter
1 tablespoon mustard
2 sour pickles, sliced
dash of pepper

Cut off one end of the bread, and remove the insides with a large spoon. Cut the removed bread into ½-inch cubes, and place in large bowl. Sprinkle milk onto the bread cubes. In another bowl, mix sour cream, eggs, ham, butter, mustard, pickles, and pepper. Add bread cubes and mix thoroughly. Stuff the mixture into the bread crust, and place in refrigerator for 1 hour. Cut bread into 1-inch slices, and serve as side dish.

MAKES 10 SERVINGS

UNLEAVEN BREAD
(Lokša)

½ cup flour
3 cups mashed potatoes
3 tablespoons butter

Blend flour into mashed potatoes making a non-sticky dough.
Divide dough into 4 portions. Roll out each portion on a
floured board to an 8-inch circle about ⅛ inch thick. Stick a
fork all over the surfaces to prevent puffing. Preheat oven to
400°F. Place dough on cookie sheets and bake on bottom rack
for 7 minutes on each side. Brush butter on bread, cut into
wedges, and serve. Good with soups and salads.

MAKES 16 SERVINGS

BRATISLAVA CRESCENTS
(Bratislavské Rožky)

3½ cups flour
dash of salt
2 egg yolks
1 cup sugar
1 package dry yeast
2 sticks (1 cup) butter
½ cup milk

FILLING:
1 cup chopped nuts
½ cup milk
1 egg

In a large bowl, add flour, salt, egg yolks, sugar, yeast, butter, and milk, and mix into a uniform dough. Cover bowl, and place in warm, draft-free space for 4 hours. Place dough on a floured board and gently roll until about ½ inch thick. Cut into 2-inch by 2-inch squares. Prepare the filling in a small pot, by adding nuts and milk and cooking for 10 minutes. Let filling cool, then spoon onto squares. Roll squares into crescent shapes, place on baking sheet, and store overnight in refrigerator. Preheat oven to 325°F. Beat egg, baste crescents, and bake for 25 minutes.

MAKES 16 PIECES

Recipe Index

Desserts & Breads, 91
Apple Fritters (Jablká V
  Župane), 93
Apple Strudel (Jablková
  Štrudla), 94
Braided Bread (Bábovka), 128
Bratislava Crescents
  (Bratislavské Rožky), 133
Chestnut Puree (Gaštanové
  Pyré), 100
Christmas Dumplings
  (Bobálky), 129
Cottage Cheese Bread Cake
  (Tvarohová Žeml'ovka), 125
Cottage Cheese Dough Balls
  (Tvarohové Knedličky), 126
Cottage Cheese Dumplings
  (Syrove Buchty), 127
Delicate Apple Cake (Krehký
  Jablčník), 96
Dobosh Torte (Dobošová
  Torta), 97
Easter Bread (Paska), 130
Fanky (Čeregy), 101
Fruit Cake (Ovocné Koláče), 102

Honey Cookies
  (Medovníky), 103
Jam Crisscross Cookies
  (Ovocné Kekse), 104
Jelly Cakes (Lekvarove
  Kolácky), 107
Kava Cake (Kávová Torta), 109
Marzipan (Marcipán), 111
Nut Roll (Orechovník), 112
Pancakes with Cottage Cheese
  (Palacinky So Syrom), 114
Plum Tarts (Slivkové
  Knedličky), 115
Poppy Seed Cake (Makový
  Kolác), 116
Poppy Seed Cookies (Makové
  Kekse), 105
Poppy Seed Dumplings
  (Makové Buchty), 117
Prune Cake (Slivkový
  Koláč), 119
Punch Cake (Punčová
  Torta), 120
Rice Pudding (Ryžový
  Nákyp), 123

Slovak Donuts (Šišky), 124
Stuffed Bread (Plnený
  Chlieb), 131
Unleaven Bread (Lokša), 132
Vanilla Wafer Cake (Vanilova
  Torta), 122
Walnut Cookies (Orechové
  Kekse), 106
Walnut Torte (Orechová
  Torta), 99

Main Dishes, 51
Baked Goose (Pečená Hus), 53
Beef Birds (Hovädzie
  Vtáčky), 73
Beef Roulder (Mäsová
  Roláda), 74
Beef with Sour Cream and
  Mushrooms (Hovädzie z
  Smotanou a Hríbami), 75
Beef with Vegetables
  (Hovädzie na Zelenine), 76
Breaded Chicken (Vypražaná
  Sliepka), 55
Broiled Liver (Grilovaná
  Pečienka), 83
Cabbage-Ham-Noodle
  Casserole (Kapusta S
  Šunkou A Slížami), 59
Chicken Livers with Rice
  (Slepačia Pečienka s
  Ryžou), 58
Chicken Paprika (Slepačí
  Paprikaš), 56

Country Beef (Hovädzie
  Nadivo), 77
Deep-Fried Pork Chops
  (Vyprážaný Rezeň), 65
Fish Patties (Rybacie
  Karbonátky), 87
Fish Ragu (Rybacie Ragú), 88
Fried Liver (Vypráňaná
  Pečeň), 84
Goulash (Gulás), 85
Ham Rolls (Šunkovy
  Závitok), 60
Jellied Pig's Feet
  (Huspenina), 62
Kielbasa with Sauerkraut and
  Potatoes (Klobasy s Kyslou
  Kapustou a Zemiakmi), 63
Marinated Fish (Marinovaná
  Ryba), 89
Meat Balls (Fašírky), 79
Nitra Delicatessen (Nitrianska
  Pochút'ka), 57
Pieštany Cutlet (Piešt'anský
  Rezeň), 68
Pork Chop Sandwich
  (Bravcový Sandvic), 66
Pork Loin with Sauerkraut
  (Bravčové S Kapustou), 67
Roast Duck (Pečená Kačica), 54
Sauerkraut Goulash (Kapustný
  Guláš), 86
Shepherd's Kielbasa
  (Bačovská Klobasa), 64
Slovak Meat Loaf (Fašírka), 80
Sour Beef (Mäso Na Kyslo), 78

Spiš Meat Delicacy (Spišská Pochút'ka), 69
Stuffed Cabbage Rolls (Plnená Kapusta), 81
Stuffed Peppers (Plnené Papriky), 82
Veal Rissoto (Rizoto), 70
Veal Stew with Dumplings (Telací Guláš s Knedlou), 71
Zvolen Smoked Ham (Zvolen Údené), 61

Soups, 1
Barley Soup (Jačmenova Polievka), 4
Beef Soup (Hovädzia Polievka), 24
Beet Soup (Cviklova Polievka), 5
Caraway Seed Soup (Kmínova Polievka), 6
Cauliflower Soup (Karfiolová Polievka), 7
Celery Soup (Zelerová Polievka), 8
Chicken Vegetable Soup with Dumplings (Slepačia Polievka s Knedličkami), 22
Dill Soup (Koprová Polievka), 9
Dry Bean Soup (Fazul'ova Polievka), 19
Fish Soup (Rybacia Polievka), 26
Garlic Soup (Cesnaková Polievka), 21

Green Bean Soup (Fresh) (Stručková Fazulová Polievka), 17
Ham Bone Pea Soup (Hrachova Polievka), 25
Kale Soup (Kelová Polievka), 11
Kohlrabi Soup (Kalerábova Polievka), 12
Lentil Soup (Šošovicova Polievka), 20
Mushroom Soup (Hríbova Polievka), 10
Natural Vegetable Soup (Prírodná Zeleninová Polievka), 18
Onion Soup with Cottage Cheese (Cibul'ová S Syrom), 15
Potato Soup (Zemiakova Polievka), 16
Slovak Soup Sauce (Zapražka), 3
Sour Cabbage Soup (Kysla Kapustná Polievka), 13
Tomato Soup (Paradajkova Polievka), 14

Vegetables & Side Dishes, 27
Apples with Horseradish (Jablká S Chrenom), 29
Baked Cauliflower (Pečený Karfiol), 30
Deep-Fried Cauliflower (Vyprážaný Karfiol), 31

Deep-Fried Cheese
(Vyprážaný Syr), 32
Dumplings (Halušky), 34
Dumplings with Feta Cheese
(Bryndzové Halučky), 35
Easter Cheese (Veľkonočný
Syr), 33
Egg Noodles (Slíže), 37
Fried Lettuce (Vyprážaný
Šalát), 38
Layered Potato Casserole
(Nakladané Zemiaky), 39
Mushroom Paprikas (Hríbový
Paprikáš), 43

Pagach (Pagáč), 44
Pirogis (Pirohy), 46
Potato Dumplings (Zemiakova
Knedla), 36
Potato Pancakes (Zemiakova
Baba), 40
Potato Salad (Zemiakový
Šalát), 41
Potato Stew (Zemiakový
Guláš), 42
Salsa with Eggs (Lešo S
Vajcami), 48
Sweet and Sour Cabbage
(Kyslo Sladká Kapusta), 49

Slovak Dictionaries from HIPPOCRENE . . .

Slovak-English/English-Slovak Dictionary and Phrasebook
by Sylvia & John Lorinc
Slovak is spoken by 4½ million people in Slovakia, 100,000 in the U.S. and is the second of the two official languages in the Czech Republic. This dictionary and phrasebook, written to help travelers and businesspeople, features an extensive vocabulary, a useful introduction to Slovak grammar and important phrases for getting around.
1,300 entries • 3¾ x 7 • 0-7818-0663-1 • $13.95pb • (754)

Slovak-English/English-Slovak Concise Dictionary
7,500 entries • 4 x 6 • 0-87052-115-2 • $11.95pb • (390)

Slovak-English/English-Slovak Compact Dictionary
7,500 entries • 3½ x 4¾ • 0-7818-0501-5 • $8.95pb • (107)

Slovak Handy Extra Dictionary
3,000 entries • 5½ x 8¼ • 0-7818-0101-X • $12.95pb • (359)

Other Cookbooks of Interest from HIPPOCRENE . . .

The Best of Czech Cooking
Peter Trnka
Although similar to the cuisines of Russia, Hungary and Poland, Czech cooking is uniquely delicious. It is a cuisine at once practical and elegant. While meat dishes are most often the centerpiece of Czech meals, a variety of delicious soups, salads, dumplings, vegetables, and desserts are also popular. This book, with over 200 recipes, is an excellent introduction to the dishes that form the basis of Czech cooking.
248 pages • 5 x 8½ • 0-7818-0492-2 • $12.95pb • (376)

All Along the Danube
Recipes from Germany, Austria, Czechoslovakia, Yugoslavia, Hungary, Romania, and Bulgaria
Marina Polvay
For novices and gourmets, this unique cookbook offers a tempting variety of over 300 Central European recipes from the shores of the

Danube River, bringing Old World flavor to today's dishes.
349 pages • 5½ x 8½ • numerous b/w photos & illustrations
• 0-7818-0098-6 • $14.95pb • (491)

The Art of Lithuanian Cooking

Maria Gieysztor de Gorgey
This volume of over 150 authentic Lithuanian recipes includes such classic favorites as Fresh Cucumber Soup, Lithuanian Meat Pockets, Hunter's Stew, Potato Zeppelins, as well as delicacies like Homemade Honey Liqueur and Easter Gypsy Cake. The author's introduction and easy step-by-step instructions ensure that even novice cooks can create authentic, delicious Lithuanian recipes.
230 pages • 5½ x 8½ • 0-7818-0610-7 • $24.95hc • (722)

Best of Albanian Cooking

Klementina and R. John Hysa
These 100 recipes cover every aspect of the Albanian meal, with sections on inviting meze-s (appetizers) and turshi-s (pickles) through Meat, Poultry and Rabbit, Vegetables, Soups, Fish, Pasta and Pies, Sauces, Compotes and Desserts, and Drinks. Also included are classic dishes like hearty tavë kosi (Baked Lamb with Yogurt), delicately seasoned Midhje në verë të bardhë (Mussels in White Wine), and Thëllëzë me ullinj (Grouse and Olives), all adapted for the North American kitchen.
168 pages • 5½ x 8½ • 0-7818-0609-7 • $22.50hc • (721)

Taste of Romania, Expanded Edition

Nicolae Klepper
Now updated with a chapter of Romanian-Jewish Recipes!
"A brilliant cultural and culinary history . . . a collection of recipes to be treasured, tested and enjoyed."
　　　　　　—George Lang, owner of Café des Artistes
" . . . dishes like creamy cauliflower soup, sour cream-enriched *mamaliga* (the Romanian polenta), lamb stewed in sauerkraut juice and scallions, and *mititei* (exactly like the ones I tasted so long ago in Bucharest) are simple and appealing . . . Klepper paints a pretty picture of his native country's culinary possibilities."
　　　　　　—Colman Andrews, *Saveur* magazine
A real taste of both Old World and modern Romanian culture. More

than 140 recipes, including the specialty dishes of Romania's top chefs, are intermingled with fables, poetry, photos and illustrations in this comprehensive and well-organized guide to Romanian cuisine.
335 pages • 6 x 9 • photos/illustrations • 0-7818-0766-2 • $24.95hc • (462)

Traditional Bulgarian Cooking
Atanas Slavov
This collection of over 125 authentic recipes, the first comprehensive Bulgarian cookbook published in English, spans the range of home cooking: including many stews and hearty soups using lamb or poultry and grilled meats, vegetables and cheese pastries; deserts of sweet-meats rich in sugar and honey, puddings, and dried fruit compotes.
200 pages • 5½ x 8½ • 0-7818-0581-3 • $22.50hc • (681)

The Art of Hungarian Cooking, Revised edition
Paul Pogany Bennett and Velma R. Clark
Whether you crave Chicken Paprika or Apple Strudel, these 222 authentic Hungarian recipes inlude a vast array of national favorites, from appetizers through desserts. Now updated with a concise guide to Hungarian wines!
225 pages • 5½ x 8½ • 18 b/w drawings • 0-7818-0586-4 • $11.95pb • (686)

Polish Heritage Cookery, Illustrated edition
Robert & Maria Strybel
New illustrated edition of a bestseller with 20 color photographs! Over 2,200 recipes in 29 categories, written especially for Americans!
"An encyclopedia of Polish Cookery and a wonderful thing to have!"
—*Julia Child, Good Morning America*
"*Polish Heritage Cookery* is the best [Polish] cookbook printed on the English market!"   —*Polish American Cultural Network*
915 pages • 7½ x 9½ • 16 pages color photographs • 0-7818-0558-9 • $39.95hc • (658)

The Best of Polish Cooking, Revised edition
Karen West
"A charming offering of Polish cuisine with lovely woodcuts throughout."
—*Publishers Weekly*

"Ethnic cuisine at it's best."—*The Midwest Book Review*
219 pages • 5½ x 8¼ • 0-87052-123-3 • $8.95pb • (391)

Old Warsaw Cookbook
Rysia
Includes 850 mouthwatering Polish recipes.
300 pages • 5½ x 8¼ • 0-87052-932-3 • $12.95pb • (536)

Old Polish Traditions in the Kitchen and at the Table
A cookbook and history of Polish culinary customs. Short essays cover subjects like Polish hospitality, holiday traditions, even the exalted status of the mushroom. The recipes are traditional family fare.
304 pages • 6 x 9 • 0-7818-0488-4 • $11.95pb • (546)

Best of Austrian Cuisine
Elisabeth Mayer-Browne
Nearly 200 recipes from Austria's rich cuisine: roasted meats in cream sauces, hearty soups and stews, tasty dumplings, and, of course, the pastries and cakes that remain Vienna's trademark.
224 pages • 5 x 8½ • 0-7818-0526-0 • $11.95pb • (633)

A Belgian Cookbook
Juliette Elkon
A celebration of the regional variations found in Belgian cuisine.
224 pages • 5½ x 8½ • 0-7818-0461-2 • $12.95pb • (535)

Celtic Cookbook: Traditional Recipes from the Six Celtic Lands Brittany, Cornwall, Ireland, Isle of Man, Scotland and Wales
Helen Smith-Twiddy
This collection of over 160 recipes from the Celtic world includes traditional, yet still popular dishes like Rabbit Hoggan and Gwydd y Dolig (Stuffed Goose in Red Wine).
200 pages • 5½ x 8½ • 0-7818-0579-1 • $22.50hc • (679)

The Scottish-Irish Pub & Hearth Cookbook
Kay Shaw Nelson
In this collection of 170 recipes of the best of Scottish and Irish pub fare and home cooking, you'll find old classics like Corned Beef 'N

Cabbage, Cock-A-Leekie, Avalon Apple Pie, and Fish and Chips, as well as new recipes sure to become family favorites: Tobermory Smoked Salmon Pâté, Raisin Walnut Porridge, and Skibbereen Scallop-Mushroom Pie among others.

278 pages • 5½ x 8½ • b/w photos and illustrations • 0-7818-0741-7 • $24.95hc • (164)

Traditional Recipes from Old England

Arranged by country, this charming classic features the favorite dishes and mealtime customs from across England, Scotland, Wales and Ireland.

128 pages • 5 x 8½ • 0-7818-0489-2 • $9.95pb • (157)

The Art of Irish Cooking

Monica Sheridan

Nearly 200 recipes for traditional Irish fare.

166 pages • 5½ x 8½ • 0-7818-0454-X • $12.95pb • (335)

Art of Dutch Cooking

C. Countess van Limburg Stirum

This attractive volume of 200 recipes offers a complete cross section of Dutch home cooking, adapted to American kitchens. A whole chapter is devoted to the Dutch Christmas, with recipes for unique cookies and candies that are a traditional part of the festivities.

192 pages • 5½ x 8½ • illustrations • 0-7818-0582-1 • $11.95pb • (683)

Traditional Food from Scotland: The Edinburgh Book of Plain Cookery Recipes

A delightful assortment of Scottish recipes and helpful hints for the home—this classic volume offers a window into another era.

336 pages • 5½ x 8 • 0-7818-0514-7 • $11.95pb • (620)

Traditional Food from Wales

Bobby Freeman

Welsh food and customs through the centuries. This book combines over 260 authentic, proven recipes with cultural and social history

332 pages • 5½ x 8½ • 0-7818-0527-9 • $24.95hc • (638)

Best of Scandinavian Cooking: Danish, Norwegian and Swedish
Shirley Sarvis and Barbara Scott O'Neil
This exciting collection of 100 recipes, each dish the favorite of a Scandinavian cook, spans the range of home cooking—appetizers, soups, omelets, pancakes, meats and pastries.
142 pages • 5 x 8½ • 0-7818-0547-3 • $9.95pb • (643)

The Best of Finnish Cooking
Taimi Previdi
Two hundred easy to follow recipes covering all courses of the meal, along with menu suggestions and cultural background for major holidays and festivities such as Mayday and Midsummer.
242 pages • 5 x 8½ • Bilingual index • 0-7818-0493-0 • $12.95pb • (601)

The Art of Turkish Cooking
Nesret Eren
"Her recipes are utterly mouthwatering, and I cannot remember a time when a book so inspired me to take pot in hand."
  —Nika Hazelton, *The New York Times Book Review*
308 pages • 5½ x 8½ • 0-7818-0201-6 • $12.95pb • (162)

All prices subject to change without prior notice. To purchase Hippocrene Books contact your local bookstore, call (718) 454-2366, or write to: HIPPOCRENE BOOKS, 171 Madison Avenue, New York, NY 10016. Please enclose check or money order, adding $5.00 shipping (UPS) for the first book and $.50 for each additional book.